Routledge Revivals

Aspects of a Changing Social Structure

Originally published in 1937, *Aspects of a Changing Social Structure* presents several lectures delivered in 1936 on behalf of the Sir Halley Stewart Trust. These lectures focus on discussing the interest that government was beginning to take in Britain's social welfare and industrial patterns. Topics covered include nutrition, child welfare, housing and health in relation to individuals and the state as well as new developments in industrial organisation and the future of the agricultural and coal industry. This title will be of interest to students of Sociology and History.

Aspects of a Changing Social Structure

Sir Percy Alden

ROUTLEDGE REVIVALS
Routledge
Taylor & Francis Group

First published in 1937
by George Allen & Unwin Ltd

This edition first published in 2016 by Routledge
2 Park Square, Milton Park, Abingdon, Oxon, OX14 4RN
and by Routledge
711 Third Avenue, New York, NY 10017

Routledge is an imprint of the Taylor & Francis Group, an informa business

Publisher's Note
The publisher has gone to great lengths to ensure the quality of this reprint but points out that some imperfections in the original copies may be apparent.

Disclaimer
The publisher has made every effort to trace copyright holders and welcomes correspondence from those they have been unable to contact.

A Library of Congress record exists under LC control number: 37022213

ISBN 13: 978-1-138-96329-0 (hbk)
ISBN 13: 978-1-315-65886-5 (ebk)
ISBN 13: 978-1-138-96330-6 (pbk)

SIR HALLEY STEWART LECTURE, 1936

THE
SIR HALLEY STEWART TRUST

★

FOUNDED 15TH DECEMBER 1924
FOR RESEARCH TOWARDS THE CHRISTIAN IDEAL IN ALL SOCIAL LIFE.

The objects of the Trust are *in general:*

To advance religion; to advance education; to relieve poverty; to promote other Charitable purposes beneficial to the community, and *in particular:*

1. To assist in the discovery of the best means by which "the mind of Christ" may be applied to extending the Kingdom of God by the prevention and removal of human misery;
2. To assist in the study of our Lord's life and teaching in their explicit and implicit application to the social relationships of man;
3. To express the mind of Christ in the realization of the Kingdom of God upon earth and in a national and a world-wide brotherhood;

For example:

For every Individual, by furthering such favourable opportunities of education, service, and leisure as shall enable him or her most perfectly to develop the body, mind, and spirit:

In all Social Life, whether domestic, industrial, or national, by securing a just environment, and

In International Relationships, by fostering good will between all races, tribes, peoples, and nations so as to secure the fulfilment of the hope of "peace on earth";

4. To provide fees for a Lecture or Lectures annually and prizes for essays or other written compositions, and to pay for their publication and distribution;
5. To provide, maintain, and assist Lectures and Research work in Social, Economic, Psychological, Medical, Surgical, or Educational subjects;
6. To make grants to Libraries;
7. To assist publications exclusively connected with the objects of the Trust (not being newspapers or exclusively denominational);
8. To make grants to and co-operate with Societies, Organizations, and Persons engaged in the furtherance of Charitable objects similar to the objects of the Trust;
9. To use the foregoing and any such other methods whether of a like nature or not, as are lawful and reasonable and appropriate for the furtherance of the objects of the Trust.

The income of the Trust may not be used for dogmatic, theological or ecclesiastical purposes other than the cult of the Science of God as manifest in man in the Son of Man in the person and teaching of our Lord, "The Word of God," Who "liveth and abideth forever."

PREVIOUS HALLEY STEWART LECTURES
Published at 4s. 6d. net each

1926

Science and Human Progress

By Sir OLIVER LODGE

"A valuable work, courageous, comprehensive, and simply expressed."—*Quarterly Review*
Third Impression

1927

Christ and Society

By Bishop GORE, D.D., LL.D.

"With the zeal of a prophet Dr. Gore recalls his fellow-disciples to the first principles of Christian faith and fellowship."—*Times Literary Supplement*
Second Impression. Also in Paper, 2s. 6d. net.

1928

The Ordeal of this Generation

By GILBERT MURRAY, LL.D., D.Litt.

"The reader will be dull indeed who does not appreciate the beautiful coherence of argument."—*Times Literary Supplement* *Third Impression*

1929

Equality

By R. H. TAWNEY, D.Litt.

"The dignified beauty of its style, the wide range of its knowledge, the serried vigour of its argument, make it a contribution of high importance to social theory." —H. J. Laski in the *Week-end Review* *Revised Cheaper Second Edition*

1930

Health and Social Evolution

By SIR GEORGE NEWMAN, K.C.B., M.D., F.R.C.P., LL.D.

"Bears on every page the stamp of expert knowledge, generous humanism, and the broadest literary culture."—*British Weekly*

1931

The World's Economic Crisis

and the Way of Escape

By Sir ARTHUR SALTER, Sir JOSIAH STAMP, J. M. KEYNES, Sir BASIL BLACKETT, Sir W. H. BEVERIDGE, HENRY CLAY

"Rarely have economic problems been so lucidly outlined."—*John o' London's Weekly*
Third Impression

1932

From Chaos to Control

By Sir NORMAN ANGELL

"Enforces its points with a pungent effectiveness that claims for it a wide audience." —*Manchester Guardian*

1933

The Way to Social Peace

By WICKHAM STEED

"Brings the European experience of a life-time to bear on the social problem of the age."—*Times*

1934

Is War Obsolete?

By Canon C. E. RAVEN, D.D.

"I have rarely seen the difficulty more fearlessly faced than in this honest and straightforward book."—*Spectator*

1935

Scientific Progress

By Sir JAMES JEANS, F.R.S., Sir WILLIAM BRAGG, O.M., F.R.S., Professor E. V. APPLETON, F.R.S., Professor E. MELLANBY, F.R.S., Professor J. B. S. HALDANE, F.R.S., and Professor JULIAN HUXLEY

(This Lecture is published at *7s. 6d.*)

ASPECTS OF A CHANGING SOCIAL STRUCTURE

SIR HALLEY STEWART LECTURE, 1936

ASPECTS OF A CHANGING SOCIAL STRUCTURE

by

Sir Percy Alden, M.A.

LONDON
George Allen & Unwin Ltd
MUSEUM STREET

FIRST PUBLISHED IN 1937

PRINTED IN GREAT BRITAIN BY
UNWIN BROTHERS LTD., WOKING

CONTENTS

PREFACE

Some apology is needed for the isolated character of the articles contained in this volume. Perhaps a more unifying title for these disconnected lectures would have been "Some Basic Social and Industrial Problems." Four chapters consist of lectures delivered in the autumn of last year on subjects that specially concern the Ministry of Health. They were an attempt to show the ever-increasing interest which Government departments are taking in problems of social welfare, and Sir Kingsley Wood, who occupied the chair at the first lecture, laid emphasis on the fact that his Ministry viewed the problems of nutrition and child welfare, of housing, and health, as vitally important both to the individual and to the State. Doubtless such increasing interest on the part of the Government necessarily implies a certain measure of State control, but so far as the Ministry of Health is concerned, while giving more assistance, no attempt is made to encroach upon the domain of the local authorities. The three links in the chain of remedial and constructive action are the State, the municipality, and voluntary social service, and if these four lectures fail to make that relationship manifest they have not carried out the purpose of the lecturer.

The other chapters deal with new developments in industrial organization and the future of certain basic industries.

The Future of the Coal and the Agricultural Industries were chosen as subjects because it is in these two industries that we shall expect in the near future great changes and because at the same time in a very real sense they are the basis of all our industrial life. In ever-increasing degree the State is exercising control in these two industries. We must expect to see a regulation of prices, of sales, and productive capacity. The coal-mining industry lies at the very root of the entire British industrial system. It is therefore a matter of concern to all consumers, whether domestic or industrial, that coal should be produced as efficiently as possible and sold at the lowest possible price consonant with the necessity for the maintenance of profits. Definite legislative action has been taken which will in the end test the efficiency of controlled competition.

In agriculture again the establishment of control could only be explained in reference to post-war developments. The depression in agriculture at home and the changes in agricultural policy abroad make it inevitable that the State should intervene. Disorganized markets and falling prices determined the action that the Board of Agriculture was compelled to take. It is not merely the farmer who has to be considered, but the country as a whole must attain a higher degree of self-sufficiency in view of the possibility of war and of a food shortage. Neither can the problem of unemployment be ignored in this connection, for with hundreds of thousands of miners idle, with hundreds of thousands of acres derelict, it was inevitable that the Government should turn its attention to more constructive measures less open to criticism than wholesale unemployment insurance.

The underlying purpose, therefore, of these lectures may be said to be the growing interest of the State in Social and Industrial Problems leading to a wide range of measures designed to give security to the citizen and to the basic industries upon which in the end both citizen and the State depend.

ASPECTS OF A CHANGING SOCIAL STRUCTURE

CHAPTER I

THE CHILD—THE FUTURE CITIZEN

Only the narrowest and most prejudiced survey can be blind to the evils and the antinomies of modern life. Immeasurable tracts of wealth go cheek by jowl with wastes of immeasurable poverty. We have playgrounds where there are no longer children, and we have children where there are no longer playgrounds. We have proved the command of man over nature, but only to demonstrate the tyranny of man over man.

REGINALD A. BRAY

THERE can be no solution of the many problems connected with social and community welfare unless we begin at the beginning. The child is the foundation of the State and the first line of defence. We cannot lay too much stress upon the importance of the child if the State is to endure. We must therefore encourage every measure which makes for its physical well being. In theory all nations have held since Plato's day that healthy and well-bred children were a valuable asset, but few nations have taken the requisite steps to ensure that the child is not a wasting asset. In some countries there is a declining birth rate, in others where the birth rate is high great carelessness is displayed with regard to child nutrition and up-bringing. In our own country theory has long ago outstripped practice. Our doctors, our educationalists, our social reformers, our eugenists are continually urging the State to secure more completely the proper education, training and nutrition of boys and girls.

While we must admit with the Board of Education and the Ministry of Health that great strides have been made, we must still deplore the fact that we do not take a more complete and scientific view of the child problem. The rapid expansion of our Empire and the growth in our material wealth tend to obscure the immediate problems connected with the making of citizens. We have forgotten that, if the increase in our material wealth is not accompanied by a corresponding increase in the well-being of the working classes, if we are neglecting the underfed children and the children who often live in unhealthy and degrading conditions, we are building upon very insecure foundations. The best returns of a nation's wealth are not always realized in hard cash. It is not too late to combat the evils that have been so long unchecked and unhindered, but there should be no further delay in organizing all the forces of our civilization with a view to creating, even for the poorest child in the realm, such an environment as will make him fit to play his part as a member of this great democracy. We all know the tradition that "an Englishman's home is his castle," but if his castle consists of one or two poorly furnished rooms in an overcrowded and verminous tenement, he is hardly likely to be proud of it, or to provide what is needful for the upbringing of his children. Cleanliness may be next to Godliness, but it is next to impossible in such conditions. We can trace the defective condition of school children to the great army of the poor in the slums of our big cities, and of these people we may say that we need wisdom most when dealing with people who possess it least.

The child is so important that it is worth while considering what can be done with regard to the decrease in child population. It is true that infant mortality has dropped from 105 per thousand births in 1910 to 57 per thousand in 1936, but nevertheless what is happening is that the predominantly young population which has existed in this country for so long is gradually disappearing. The latest calculations seem to prove that by 1941 the population of Great Britain will have decreased from 45,000,000, at which it probably stands today, to 44,800,000. In 1951 it is estimated that the figures will be about 42,500,000, followed by a further rate of contraction, so that for 1966 the estimate of population is 37,500,000. A dwindling population means that every child is potentially more valuable to the community if it is reared to become a healthy citizen.

It is not merely the decrease in population that is a matter of concern; in some respects, that might become an advantage. The trouble is that the number of aged people is increasing out of all proportion to the rest of the population, while the number of young people is decreasing. Meanwhile more than half the people in Great Britain are now over thirty, and within fifty years it seems likely that more than half will be over forty years of age. In 1901 in Great Britain there were 12,000,000 children up to fifteen years of age; in 1931 they had decreased by 1,000,000; and it is estimated that by 1951 there will only be 6,500,000. At the beginning of this century children outnumbered adults of sixty-five by 7 to 1. The tendency is now all the other way. Although, therefore, the expectation of life has increased and more children survive until maturity, the birth rate would still be too low to maintain the population at its present level. Every year's decline in births in future will be reflected increasingly in reductions of the population in forty years' time, since the number of younger adults is near its peak. As the population grows older a rising fertility rate will be necessary to prevent the population from falling with accelerated speed. It is true that all these estimates may be to some extent falsified by changes that may still take place. It is just possible that a period of prosperity might mean a greatly increased birth rate, or a marked change in the feeling with regard to birth control might imply that the practice of family limitation had declined. But taking the figures as they stand, although infant mortality is declining together with the general death rate, we still are faced with the problem of how to ensure the maintenance of the child portion of the community. What is required is three children to the family instead of one.

The population problem is beyond the scope of this lecture, but none the less we have to bear it in mind when we are considering the importance of the child. It means that we have to save every child that is born healthy and that we have to see to it that the conditions under which the child is reared are such as will make him strong both physically and mentally. The overwhelming pressure of town life, the lack of fresh air, the tendency for the poor to crowd together in insanitary slums, the increased difficulty of obtaining a pure and cheap milk supply, the almost greater difficulty of keeping the milk free from contact with germs and filth in the home —these things have emphasized the importance of the Child Welfare Clinic. Since the Notification of Births Act of 1907 a very great advance has been made in this direction and the decrease in infant mortality is undoubtedly due to the fact that the ante-natal clinic, followed by the child welfare clinic, has meant the discovery of weaknesses or of malnutrition at a very early stage. The percentage of women who attended ante-natal clinics in relation to the number of notified births has steadily increased. Moreover, the number of local authorities that are carrying out schemes of maternity and child welfare have also increased and the returns show that the majority of the maternity and child welfare authorities supply free milk, or milk at less than cost price to nursing mothers and children. We see now why infant mortality has dropped from 105 per thousand births in 1910 to 57 in 1935. During the last fifteen years the number of infant welfare centres has practically doubled and whole time health visitors have risen from 1,607 to 6,002. Part of the improvement which is noticed in the health of young children from one to three, and from three to five, is due to the fact that milk is more generally given. It was noticed that one pint a day to small children under five years of age in a Special Area in South Wales gave unexpectedly valuable results. In fact, these children, from the point of view of nutrition, were better off than children in a neighbouring and more prosperous city in which free milk was only given during the first year of life. The value of milk as a food must be pressed home. Under the Milk in Schools Scheme the number of elementary school children paying for milk or receiving it free has increased from 900,000 in 1933 to 2,406,000 in 1936. Yet more than half the scholars in our public elementary schools are still not getting any milk, or very little, so that there is plenty of room for improvement.

In the towns situated in the Special Areas the percentage instead of being 50 or 60 or, in some cases, 87 per cent, sinks as low as 29 or 30. Not only the little children of twelve months or over should receive free milk but the local education authority should provide free milk wherever medical treatment after inspection is necessary and wherever there is any likelihood of malnutrition.

There is no doubt whatever that the milk experiment has been a great success, and that sooner or later it will be placed on a broader and more permanent basis. Those who criticize the giving of free milk to the poorer children of our community regard it as a piece of pauperization, unnecessary and demoralizing. We can remember the same argument being used in the case of Unemployment and Health Insurance Acts and Old Age Pensions. Yet we are now reconciled to the conception of these social services even though we may consider them to be imperfectly devised in the first instance. We do not any longer dispute the importance of helping the sick poor with medicine and treatment, and there is no reason in the nature of things why we should refuse to give children who are etiolated and devitalized the milk which will prevent sickness. Under the Education Act school children cannot obtain free milk unless the family income is extremely small and unless their physical state is such that they cannot otherwise benefit from education. Under the Maternity and Child Welfare Act milk is supplied free or cheap only after a means test and upon medical recommendation. Sir John Orr, who is anxious that cheap or free milk should be supplied both to mothers and to infants and school children, suggests that the cost could be met by a subsidy or by a reduction in distributive costs or a combination of the two. Whatever scheme is devised it is quite certain that we should get a real return in value for the expense incurred.

An investigation is now being carried on by the London County Council into the nutritive value of milk, by which 8,000 children are being weighed every four months. This effort, side by side with a periodical weighing and measuring of the 400,000 children under the London County Council under twelve years of age, should throw a great deal of light upon the close connection between diet and growth. A very interesting inquiry was recently made by the Medical Officer of Health for Stockton-on-Tees. In a book entitled *Poverty and Public Health*, the author traces the extent of physical unfitness among the adult male population to defects which have been shown to exist in infancy, childhood, and adolescence. Where there has been neglect in these early stages it is followed by a high proportion of disease and ill-health. The investigations extending over five years seem to show that an extremely important rôle is played by nutrition; that it is in some respects more important than environment, although no one questions the evil of living under slum conditions. If, however, nutritional processes are interfered with, if poverty or ignorance or both mean that there is a lack of proper food, there is sure to be an increased disease rate and an increased mortality. The argument, therefore, is that, unless minimum dietaries adequate to maintain health are supplied, the family will suffer, especially the mother and the children. The investigators even go so far as to say that the very poor, when they are rehoused, if by necessity they pay an increased rent, suffer in health because of a less satisfactory dietary. What does emerge from the inquiry, beyond doubt, is that death rates, disease rates, and malnutrition seem to vary in proportion to the income of the parents and that two factors of supreme importance are, first, housing conditions, and, secondly, the question of diet.

This experiment, which perhaps would not be regarded as conclusive unless it could be tried on a larger scale, is none the less an extremely valuable one within certain limits. I use the expression "within certain limits" because it appears that over 90 per cent of the families investigated after their removal to a new housing estate were unemployed and had been so, in some cases, over long periods. It does not follow that, if investigations had been carried out on other housing estates where there was less unemployment, anything like the same results would have been obtained. The areas described are the Housewife Lane area and the Riverside area, and the comparison is with the whole of Stockton-on-Tees and the whole of England and Wales. The average infant mortality rate per thousand live births during the years 1928–32 was for Stockton itself 78·8, for the Riverside area it was 134, and for the previous period of 1923–27 the Riverside area showed 173. It is not possible to give in detail all the results of this inquiry, but the statistics seem to prove that wherever you get poverty it is accompanied by malnutrition and by an increased infant mortality. As you ascend the scale of wages there is less malnutrition and a lower death rate. We have no accurate means of judging what proportion of the child population is under-nourished, but it seems likely that of the population which would be described as poor, according to the standard of the British Medical Association Inquiry, a large percentage would be malnourished. Mal-nourished children mean weakly and defective citizens, and the rejection for medical unfitness of so large a percentage of the adults coming forward as army recruits seems to show that this unfitness pursues them throughout life.

Routine medical inspection seems to emphasize this point. If we compare the figures for 1933 with those for 1913, we find considerable improvement, but the 1933 figures show, as a result of the inspection of 1,855,000 children, that 11·1 per thousand were suffering from malnutrition of a sufficient degree to require treatment, and a further 12·8 per thousand were marked for observation because of a less degree of malnutrition. The two figures give a total of 23·9 per thousand children as suffering from some degree of malnutrition. On the other hand, as a result of the new classification in 1935, when 1,687,331 children were examined and classified on the new basis, viz. on clinical grounds instead of merely height and weight, it was found that 74·1 per cent of the children were normal, 10·6 per cent slightly subnormal, and only 0·7 per cent bad. It is obvious, therefore, that there is no satisfactory definition of malnutrition at the present time. Nutrition, according to the new classification, means the nourishment or the general well-being of the child. As Sir Robert McCarrison says, "Food is the instrument, nutrition is the act of using it," and nutrition therefore depends upon sleep, sunlight, fresh air, and exercise as well as food.

It is interesting to compare the figures provided by the Newcastle investigation, made by Dr. Spence, the Medical Officer of Health. He stated that 36 per cent of the children from the poor districts were physically unfit and that they appeared malnourished. These children were compared with children from better class families and records seem to show that of the professional classes over 48 per cent were above the normal zone for weight, 38 per cent were normal, and only 12 per cent below the normal zone, whereas in the poorer districts only 11 per cent were above normal, 33 per cent within the normal zone, and 55 per cent below the normal zone. If we take the heights we find that 25 per cent of the professional classes were above the normal zone, and only 1·7 per cent of the poorer children, that only 4·8 per cent of the professional classes were below the normal zone in height and 47 per cent of the city children, as they were called, were below the zone. In the same way only 16 per cent of the professional families' children presented any degree of anaemia and on the other hand only 19 per cent of the city children were free from it. Dr. Spence came to the conclusion that there is a direct relationship between overcrowding, malnutrition, and ill-health and that, since the high incidence of apparent malnutrition is not found in the children of better-class families, it is due to preventable causes.

Going back to a previous investigation, made in 1907 by Dr. Leslie Mackenzie in Glasgow, where a comparison is made between varying grades of poverty and classifying them as those living in one-, two-, three-, or four-roomed tenements, it was shown that boys from two-roomed houses were 11·7 lb. lighter on an average than boys from four-roomed houses and 4·7 inches shorter. In the same way girls from one-roomed houses were on the average 14 lb. lighter and 5·3 inches shorter than girls from four-roomed houses. It has been contended that these figures are not satisfactory, because they cover too small a number of children, but it would be possible for the Government, while the Ministry of Labour is undertaking the new cost of living inquiry, which will require the co-operation of many thousands of housewives as well as tradesmen and property owners, to attempt by a sectional inquiry to deal with this problem, which once and for all ought to be placed on a sound basis. Supposing that we could investigate eight thousand domestic budgets of the relatively poor, we could then follow that up with an additional inquiry. What we want to know is, in the case of the comparatively poor, how many of the children are suffering from malnutrition, what are their heights and weights, and what are their measurements as compared with the normal child. If it could be shown that the wages of the parents after the payment of rent and other outgoings were insufficient to provide either the right amount or the right quality of food required, we should then have a strong case for asking that the Government should step in and deal with this problem of malnutrition on national lines.

Many of us believe that, in the case of little children, this is a question of an adequate supply of milk. It has been proved on many occasions that this is the ideal food for little children, and it is admitted that the children of the unemployed in the special areas suffer from lack of milk. The fact that free milk is available to selected children in the schools and at the clinics, and that milk at a low cost is supplied to others, does not settle the question. The question of the milk supply generally is a difficult one, but production of milk was 35 per cent in excess of consumption and we are using a very large quantity sold at a very low rate for manufacturing purposes, while hundreds of thousands of children are suffering for lack of it. The effect on something like half the child population, therefore, is not to develop normal healthy children but to weaken their power of resistance to disease. If all these children could receive a proper supply, a pint day by day, we should see a great improvement in physique and a consequent reduction in sickness and ill-health. This would be followed by a lessening of the cost of treating disease, either by public health authorities or by municipal and voluntary hospitals.

It is becoming evident on all hands that a great deal of disease could be prevented, and if suitable and adequate diet meant sound health for the young, it would be well worth while for the Ministry of Health to take up this question of nutrition in the interests of the physique of the nation. We are always talking about a glut of foodstuffs, and measures are being taken to raise prices in the interests of the farmers, but surely our first aim should be to produce strong and healthy citizens. Accordingly, the national food policy today should be based on increased consumption, since increased production seems to be well within the power of the community. Sir Josiah Stamp, in his presidential address to the British Association, made this remark: "It has been computed," he said, "that a benevolent dictator could, at a relatively small expense, by applying our modern knowledge of diet, add some 2 inches to the average stature and 7 lb. or 8 lb. to the average weight of the general population, besides enormously increasing their resistance to disease." It would seem, therefore, surveying this question from a purely materialistic or realistic point of view, that it would be to the advantage of the State to deal with this further urgent problem of a scientifically adequate diet for all the youth of the country, regarding it as a measure of defence as important as the construction of a battleship.

Most of us take a fairly optimistic view with regard to the rise in the standard of living. We believe that the average man has achieved a position in which he can be sure of a sufficiency in food and clothing and housing with some recreation during his leisure hours, but when we come to consider that large class that is either unemployed or only casually employed, it is very doubtful whether the standard of life is not tending to fall. In any poor area where there is a good deal of unemployment, and often in areas where there is little unemployment, it is clear that the people resident in these areas get only about half the average national ration of milk, and although the consumption of butter is on the increase, they probably get less than one-third of the average amount consumed throughout the country. On the other hand there is evidence that we are increasing the quantity of milk and butter and eggs either produced in this country or imported from abroad. This seems to imply that some classes of the community are getting far more than they need and others are getting less. As the physical comes first in point of time and perhaps in point of importance as the basis of all progress, it is clearly necessary that we should make sure that every household has at least the minimum food allowance that will make for the building up of the body. My experience for what it is worth is that children are often underfed in homes where you would least expect it and in almost every case it seems to be due to the fact that the parents, in their anxiety to keep up a respectable appearance, are paying too much in rent and are therefore unable to feed their children adequately. It is not only the question of rent, there is the question of clothes, of washing materials, of everything that makes for cleanliness. Sometimes the dirtiest and most ragged children are the best fed because so little money has been spent on anything but food.

The experience of Dr. M'Gonigle at Stockton-on-Tees that the death rate on the new estates was increasing and the health of the occupants not improving, because they were spending too much money on rent and not enough on food, is probably exceptional. Put in another way his contention is that in the slum area from which they were evacuated, the rent was not so high as to deprive them of necessary food. We need not question the accuracy of Dr. M'Gonigle's figures and if he says that "the average rents of the new housing estate were nearly double those of the previous slum area," there is nothing to be done but to deplore it and to urge that some change should be made. You cannot expect a family to live upon an average of 2s. 10½d. per head per week! On the other hand, I have visited many new estates in which the rents are not appreciably higher than those in the slum area and in those cases there ought to be an increase in health and a similar decrease in the death rate. My own view is that, taking the country as a whole, it will be found that the housing campaign has had a marked effect upon the health of the children. Still, this does not affect the argument that in a large number of cases lack of sufficient nourishing food, due to poverty, has led to an inability to resist disease, and whether it is infant mortality or the general death rate, malnutrition is bound to have its effect. It will have its effect in later life even if it does not show itself in the early days. What happens is a slow sapping of vitality which makes a speedy recovery from disease impossible. A child cannot be killed quickly by ill-feeding, but if he is badly nourished it means loss of health, a tendency to disease and an earlier death. We have had various reports as to the condition of children in the special areas and it is difficult to say that the children are suffering greatly. The trouble is that so many of the diseases of later life lie latent and come to the front when the body, exhausted by malnutrition, is incapable of resistance. It has been shown that if you start with malnourished children and feed them as they should be fed, especially with a sufficient quantity of milk, they will increase in height and weight faster than a normal child and will reduce the deficiency in six or seven months by as much as 40 per cent, but during the next year the feeding with an adequate supply of milk does not produce the same effect. They will increase at the normal rate both in height and in weight, but they are never able to make good the remainder of the deficiency. If it were possible to take the subsequent history of these children and to follow them year by year, we should probably find that though evil results were mitigated, there is always the tendency to a setback and that the standard of health was not so high amongst these children or adolescents as amongst other sections of the population.

The Medical Research Council has given us a study of nutrition, made by Cathcart and Murray, in which the amount of food required is estimated according to its calorie value. Without going into these figures, which are now regarded as accurate, it is seen that a child of from three to six years required about half as much food as a man, and a boy or girl of fourteen as much as a man or woman. The cost of this, according to Professor Bowley, in the *New Survey of London*, is for a child of five to fourteen years 2s. 10d., and for a child of fourteen to sixteen 4s. 10d., which is also the estimated cost of food for a woman. A man is put on a higher scale and in this estimate it is 5s. 8d.; other estimates require a man to spend as much as 7s. or 7s. 6d. a week. In any case the main point is that little children do not get and cannot get, when the wage is small, the pint of milk which is recommended per day and which will cost an extra 2s. a week. It is important that we should remember that children of different ages have varying needs and it is therefore quite impossible to estimate the exact amount required per child.

In the Report of the Committee set up under the chairmanship of Professor Bowley in 1913 to determine a minimum cost of different diets at different ages it was stated with regard to the child, "a supply of at least one pint of cow's milk per child per day is considered essential for adequate growth." The Report goes on to say, in estimating the minimum cost of diets for children, it is assumed that children under one year are breast fed and that from one to six years each child receives a pint of milk daily. From six to fourteen years the allowance of milk drops gradually to half a pint at ten years and a modicum of condensed milk in tea at fourteen years. The dietary suggested for children under six years of age does not allow of either butter or meat being included.

The Committee set up by the British Medical Association in 1933 to determine the minimum weekly expenditure on foodstuffs which must be incurred by families of varying size if health and working capacity are to be maintained, gave as the cost per head per week for food of the man 5s. 11d., and the boy over fourteen the same amount, and the girl over fourteen 4s. 11d., and the child of twelve and under fourteen 5s. 4d., the child of ten and under twelve 4s. 9d., and so on down to the child of two at 3s. 1d., and of one to two 2s. 8d. What arises out of all these figures is the fact that, when you take into account the cost of feeding a man and his wife and, say, three or four children, and add on the amount of the rent, the cost of fuel, of clothing, of lighting and heating, it is easy to see that a vast number of families throughout this country, owing to an insufficient wage, must either save on rent or on food, and that if they are compelled to save on food the results are disastrous.

The authors of *Poverty and Public Health* go so far as to state that two-thirds of our children are growing up under dietary conditions in which it is impossible to develop into a normal healthy adult. If the minimum standard of diet of the British Medical Association be adopted, the Stockton-on-Tees Inquiry would seem to show that the minimum standard in these areas is only obtained in the case of seven families out of 141, and if we adopt the optimum standard of Sir John Orr, nearly half the population is below the standard. It is clearly a case of what standard do we adopt and perhaps the standard is too high.

One thing seems perfectly clear: that, however much we may attribute malnutrition to ignorance, a considerable proportion of malnutrition is due to lack of a sufficient income, and we do know that as the income rises the health value of the diet improves and malnutrition decreases. The relative incidence of anaemia, brought out by a special examination of children of the professional classes in Newcastle, shows how heavily weighted the scales are against the poorer children. The normal haemoglobin level is taken to be 75 to 85 per cent. Among the children of the professional classes 16 per cent were found to be below this level as compared with 81 per cent among the children of the poor. Moreover, as we have previously stated, the death rate rises as income falls. Taking the six groups into which they divided the families in the inquiry referred to, it was found that the standardized death rate fell from nearly twenty-six per thousand in the poorest (viz. those possessing an income of 25s. to 30s. per family per week) to 11·52 in the highest incomes, viz. over 75s. per week. In the main, therefore, the excessive disease rate and death rate amongst the poorest must be due to an inadequate supply of the right foods.

If it be a fact that about half of the population of the country could be greatly improved in physique and health by improvement in the national dietary, then, as Sir Frederick Hopkins says, "A national problem of unsurpassed importance has been raised." It may be true of statistics, as it is said of science, that in any branch of investigation you must be careful not to find what you are looking for, but the weight of evidence in this case is overwhelming.

Although it was my intention to steer clear of the whole problem of education, there is one aspect of the education question which vitally affects the little child. The local education authorities are spending over £2,000,000 per annum on medical inspection and treatment met from grants and rates, and no one who has observed the immense improvement which has taken place in the physique of school children during the last twenty-five years will grudge one penny of this outlay, but continual watchfulness is necessary if we are to prevent any appreciable increase in the number of children who suffer from ill-health due to defective teeth, various forms of acute rheumatism and rickets. The need for the effective supervision of the 2,000,000 children between two and five years of age is urgent, and I know of no better way to insure that the health of these children will be watched and supervised than by the establishment of nursery schools. In the Education Act of 1918 the local authorities were given powers to establish these schools and immediate recognition was given to all that were then in existence. In 1923 twenty-six nursery schools were already established, eleven by local authorities. At present we have seventy-two nursery schools recognized by the Board of Education with places for 5,440 children. It is not suggested that all the 2,000,000 children of that age should find accommodation in nursery schools. There must be a large number, not less than 500,000, who are cared for in their own homes and under the very best conditions, with their parents. Unfortunately, however, there are on the other hand many homes that are far from ideal, where for various reasons the little child has no fair chance. Some of this is due to bad housing and some of it to crushing poverty; some of it, on the other hand, is no doubt due to the ignorance or the carelessness of the mothers, or perhaps we ought to say the parents. It seems a great deal to ask that we should supply in these cases, numbering perhaps 1,500,000, accommodation in nursery schools, especially when we remember the heavy charge already existing upon the Exchequer and the local rates. Yet if these nursery schools were available we could be sure first of all that for a considerable portion of the day the child would be cared for and watched, that it would be medically inspected and treated if defects manifested themselves, that there would be fresh air and the beginnings of intellectual development so interesting to children as to partake almost of the nature of play. Then, again, the nursery schools would make possible the provision of a midday meal at a small cost, which the parents could pay for, unless it was found desirable in certain cases that they should be free. Even with a decrease in the school child population, a large number of new schools would still be required. The cost to accommodate the children I have mentioned might be in the neighbourhood of £2,000,000, but the saving in the end would be immense, so far as disease and ill-health were concerned. It would be no small advantage that these children, taken out of their crowded homes, should have every day one nourishing meal and hours of fresh air, exercise, and sleep. It is to be hoped that they would also have their ration of sunshine, since we are apt to forget that without vitamin D a child is certain to suffer from rickets, from defective bone and teeth formation. The sunshine should, of course, be supplemented by the right kind of food, and here would come in the great advantage of the midday meal.

We might do something to help the child by clearing our atmosphere of smoke pollution, which is so injurious to health and especially in the case of little children. If we make a graph of the sunshine during each month of the year and then place under it a graph of infant mortality during those months, it will be seen that during the summer months infant mortality tends to decrease very materially, while during the winter months, especially from December to February, it shoots up again. It is not possible to be so accurate with regard to disease rates, but there is no doubt whatever that resistance to disease is greatly weakened during the winter months. Therefore, during the winter months, when there is less sunshine, it is increasingly important that children should have the right kind of diet. Given the right kind of diet and a fair ration of sunshine there is no reason in the world why rickets should not be totally abolished. It seems absurd for us to provide hospitals and homes for children suffering from rickets or surgical tuberculosis when most of the evil might be prevented if taken in time. If we could make the right start with these children they would be passed on to the elementary school unhandicapped by ill-health and ready to take advantage of the opportunities of education offered to them.

Finally, let us never forget that by saving the child you are saving the citizen and the nation. Notwithstanding the vast amount of money spent on social services there is still a huge burden to be borne by municipal and voluntary hospitals in connection with the treatment of disease. We are a humane nation, even if we are stubborn, obstinate, and short-sighted, and once convince the people in this country that the greater part of the disease from which children suffer could be prevented, undoubtedly the money would be found which is necessary to bring a diet adequate for health within the reach of the poorest families. It might conceivably be less than the cost of treating the disease itself if that disease is preventable. In some way or other the various Ministries concerned, and especially the Ministries of Education, Health, and of Agriculture, must determine whether it might not be possible to evolve a better and more satisfactory policy based on increased consumption as well as increased production. Such a policy would be in the interests of the whole community, but especially in the interests of the children to whom the nation must look in the future for citizenship and governance.

CHAPTER II

THE HEALTH OF THE CITIZEN

Over great territories of social evil, adjacent to the field of our merely medical work, we seem to see on all sides the common pervasion of one deep want, the want of riper national education. Education is the one far-reaching true reformer, for which in all the domains the sufferers have to work and hope—the education which completes for self-help and for social duty, by including wisdom and goodness; the education which teaches standards of moral right and wrong, gives height to character and aim, and applies its own hygienic discipline to the shaking-palsy of purposeless life.

SIR JOHN SIMON
English Sanitary Institution (1890)

WE have tried to show in a previous chapter that if the experts in population are right the child population in the future is bound to decrease and that therefore it is all the more important to see to it that every child that is born shall be born under hygienic conditions, is properly fed and nurtured, so that it may grow up to become a strong and healthy citizen. We have to consider, however, not only the health of the child but the health of the adult. There has been a progressive growth in medical knowledge, and our doctors and our surgeons as a whole were never so capable, so instructed, as they are today. Although the old joke "he died without medical assistance" has been dropped, there is still room for improvement both in our public medical service and in individual medical treatment. We have not yet quite passed the stage which regards medicine as being the cure or the attempt to cure a particular disease. There are too many people, including a good many doctors, inclined to choose, perhaps, what seems the easiest course, viz. to deal with the symptoms of individual disease as they see them, without attempting to get at the root causes. We are great believers in drugs, especially the poor. To a very large extent our system of Health Insurance, valuable as it has been, tends to encourage this view. It is almost too much to expect that a medical practitioner with perhaps a thousand men and women on his panel will be able to give that attention to each individual case which would not only enable him to effect a cure but also to maintain health in the future. The old idea of medicine is no doubt changing, but it is still too much wrapped up with the treatment of the patient apart from the cause of the disease and apart altogether from the environment which may either create or maintain the disease.

Nevertheless, today a new feeling is growing up with regard to health, both physical and mental. We are asking insistently what are the laws of nature to which we must conform? What is the potentiality of the body itself, in all its functions, to maintain health or restore it? What are the causes of the disease which has weakened the tissues of the body and lowered, perhaps permanently, the standard of health? The old idea was to think of the human body in parts, the part afflicted with the disease being the sole consideration, but to-day the whole of the human body is taken into account. We know now that we possess within ourselves forces which are at work with a view to maintaining health and overcoming any external attack on the fortress of life; hence the stress that is being laid today upon sunshine, fresh air, pure water, an open-air life, on proper food and clothing, on games and, generally speaking, on wholesome living.

That we have made great advances in this direction towards the conquest of disease, and perhaps ultimate victory, is shown by the gradual decrease in death rates and in disease rates. The infant mortality in 1935 was 57 per thousand live births, the lowest on record. The approximate expectation of life today as compared with a hundred years ago has very materially improved. Thus, a child who is born in England today has an expectation of life eighteen years longer than a century ago. The mortality rate for adults seems to prove that mortality has declined over 40 per cent during the same period. This is, of course, an average decline, and great variations and inequalities will be discerned when we compare the poorer classes of the community with those classes that have all the necessaries of life and some, at least, of the comforts, who have enjoyed a better education and had larger and fuller opportunities. We have stamped out certain diseases, like leprosy, plague, typhus, and scurvy. There was only one case of smallpox in 1935. No doubt other diseases have taken their place or perhaps are more fully recognized than they used to be, so we now stress the importance of the research work which is being done in the case of cancer, tuberculosis, diabetes, asthma, and many other diseases. A real attempt is being made to track down the causation of these terrors of the human body. The gains to human life can hardly be questioned. We know from our own experience, if we have lived for half a century, that there is not only a rising standard of life, but more opportunities for physical health and less direct suffering from disease. The State does more in caring for the physical well-being of its citizens, and the individual doctor has a wider outlook, believing that drugs, valuable as they may be for dealing with the symptoms of disease, are not so valuable for securing the health of the people as the observance of the laws of nature and the provision of a sound environment.

It has sometimes been contended that the provision of health services by the State and by the local authorities have tended to decrease individual responsibility, but there is very little evidence of this.

Every piece of legislation, if it is wisely administered, like maternity and infant welfare services, or the school medical service, or health insurance, or improved sanitation in housing, must have an educative tendency, and in the end conduce to the feeling of personal responsibility. No one can doubt, for example, that the child welfare clinic has encouraged and stimulated the mother in a multitude of cases to greater attention and care in the treatment of her children, watching their physical ailments and checking them in the early stages. In the same way an increase of interest on the part of the relatively poor in measures of sanitation has been noted, and if there has been any special defect in our Health Insurance system it is due not so much to the fact that there is direct monetary advantage in the number of patients as the fact that the average doctor has not the time or the energy, and sometimes not the knowledge, to make his patient understand and take the necessary steps for the cure of his disease.

The Health Insurance Act of 1911 met with a good deal of opposition when it was introduced. The doctors opposed it at the time because they conceived that it might encroach upon their special domain. As a matter of fact, it has greatly benefited the doctors in poor industrial districts. The experience, however, of over twenty years will enable us to come to some conclusions with regard to its advantages or its disadvantages. The panel doctors in England and Wales, no less than 16,000 in number, provide a health service for nearly 18,000,000 insured persons between the ages of sixteen and sixty-five, if their incomes are below £250 per annum. The benefits under the Act are administered by local insurance committees, and approved societies pay out sickness, disablement, and maternity benefits in the form of cash payments. The doctor is paid per patient. Over £400,000,000 has been paid out by approved societies in the past, since the existence of the Act. Owing to industrial depression following on the war, the original actuarial calculations proved to be defective, so that it was necessary to make the Act solvent by the National Health Insurance and Contributory Pensions Act of 1932. The payments now have reached the very large sum of over £15,000,000 per annum, with the result that every person who is insured has a claim on the practitioner for attendance and medicine within certain definite limits which are laid down. A great many doctors find it difficult to certify in accordance with their best judgment, because they fear to lose their patients. Some of them dislike to refuse certificates when the patient still complains of illness and inability to work; and it may be that in certain cases the doctor, knowing that the patient would find it impossible to obtain employment, allows sympathetic considerations to influence his judgment. We all know that what is required is prevention rather than cure. The doctor considers in many cases that he has discharged his duty in examining and giving medicine.

The system also is ineffective in so far as it fails to take advantage of the regulations of the School Medical Service, and until recently there was no medical supervision between the ages of fourteen and sixteen, so that many cases of incipient disease were overlooked. Then, again, it does not of course include medical benefits for women not gainfully employed or the dependents of insured persons, and the ideal is surely that the doctor should be aware of the conditions of the whole family and should endeavour to maintain them in health. Further, the relationship between insurance committees and approved societies, between panel doctors and the health service of the local authorities, is extremely weak unless the officials are willing to take the trouble to get into touch. There is no definite link. The approved societies merely pay out and they are in no way concerned as to whether the payment is justifiable. This question of monetary advantage to the panel doctor is not wholly satisfactory. It is part of the weakness of the system, but a still greater weakness is this lack of coherence and co-ordination on the part of authorities discharging health functions. We have, for example, district medical officers appointed under the old Poor Law, and these together with the panel doctors should surely be linked up with the services rendered by the local authority, a recommendation which was proposed by the Royal Commission of 1928. It is needless to say that there is an utter lack of uniformity in the administration of the Act by approved societies with their thousands of different branches. It is a scrappy method of dealing with the problem, and it means that those who are in greatest need are often not entitled to claim, as in the special areas or districts where sickness is most prevalent.

Taking a broad view of the whole health question, what is wanted is a periodical health examination from childhood upwards and especially should this health examination fill up the gaps which remain in the present system. If this periodical examination could be carried out by groups of doctors, some of whom would be specialists, disease would be detected in the early stages and preventive medicine would then be justified. A properly organized system would make maternity and child welfare officers responsible for the health of children under five years of age; school medical officers should take charge from that age onwards until the children leave school, and that after that the panel doctors, or at any rate some of them, might be salaried officers of the local authority and of course responsible to the Public Health Committee. It would make all the difference in the world to the possibility of success if these doctors could have the advantage of studying the records of the school children or even of the maternity and child welfare clinics. These doctors would then not wait until some disease was revealed, but they would make their periodical examinations in the same way that the school doctor does. If an insurance company in U.S.A. finds it worth while to make a free medical examination of its clients and make these inspections periodically, it is a proof that even from the monetary point of view it would pay the State. Surely it is a mistake to wait until the patient is ill enough to require a doctor or too ill to benefit by treatment. When we remember the loss of time, apart from the loss of money, represented by absence from work for 26,000,000 weeks of insured people during one year, it is sufficient evidence of the danger of delay. Fifteen years ago the loss per average worker owing to sickness was 16·5 days. Now it is 28 days a year, and sickness benefit is therefore on the increase.

The task of co-ordinating all the medical services under the local authority is a gigantic one, and we are not under-estimating the difficulty of the problem. Anyone who has had to deal with the collection of information from various sources will know how many are the delays owing to removals and changes of address, and how complicated the procedure is, requiring a vast amount of correspondence and investigation. Nevertheless, this is what is required: acquaintance not only with the history of the family, from the health point of view, but if possible the history of all the families in the area and speedy means of communication as between one section of the health service and another.

My contention receives valuable support by Sir E. Farquhar Buzzard, the President of the British Medical Association, who, in a lecture entitled "And the Future," emphasized the lack of co-ordination between all sections of the medical authorities. He said that the war against disease has been conducted on a wasteful and ill-organized system, and he praised the Ministry of Health, the Medical Research Council, and the British Medical Association for their willingness to pool their resources and to co-operate for the common good. The average doctor, he said, had insufficient time to carry out his work, which should include the prevention of disease or the detection of it in its early stages. More important still was the preservation of health, but there, of course, for various reasons the average doctor had neither opportunity nor power. If we are to maintain the present system and still carry out this work of preventive medicine, we should need 100,000 instead of 50,000 doctors and any such large increase would render it imperative that time and energy as well as money should not be wasted in any system of service. He therefore declared in favour of health centres, by which he meant a central board based geographically on the chief hospital, voluntary or municipal, as the case might be, but representative of all interests and institutions concerned with the health of the district. The duty of such a board would be to co-ordinate all the preventive and curative services within the district, to avoid overlapping and wastage, and to assure the public that its financial contributions to the common cause of health, both voluntary, State- or rate-aided, were used to the best economic advantage. Sir Farquhar Buzzard also laid great stress on the importance of institutional team work. If the saving of health, he pointed out, and the prevention of illness must be initiated by the general practitioner in the home, these practitioners should be part-time officers, helping to staff those medical services which have been diverted to the control of the public health authority. He would include in every health centre a department of research.

Many of us will differ from Sir Farquhar in regarding it possible to base the health centre on a hospital, however important that institution may be, or to regard the general practitioner, who is quite indispensable at present, as capable of taking up the work already diverted to the control of public health authorities. My own personal view is that the health centre should be based upon the Public Health Department of the local authority, in close touch with the Ministry of Health, and having upon its central board representatives of every health department or institution throughout the locality, from infant welfare upwards. The Medical Officer of Health in this case would still have a vast amount of work for which he was responsible, but his central board would be in touch with a greater variety of institutions, including tuberculosis dispensaries, orthopaedic centres, and the many-sided work of the hospitals. The greatness of this task could only be matched by its importance, but it is in this direction that we must look for the next big advance in preventive medicine.

When we are dealing with the cure of disease, as apart from prevention, we cannot praise too highly the work of our hospitals, both municipal and voluntary. The tradition in England has for many years been in favour of voluntary hospitals, contrary to what is almost the uniform practice on the continent. This tradition is in keeping with our whole idea of voluntary social service, in which respect Great Britain stands high amongst the nations of the world. The voluntary hospitals, about 1,000 in number, have done magnificent work under very difficult circumstances. They came into existence hundreds of years ago; for example, St. Bartholomew's in 1546 and St. Thomas's in 1563, two illustrations of what we may call first-class hospitals. The voluntary hospitals in London and throughout the country were originally, and are now to a large extent, charitable institutions depending upon the gifts of charitable people. They have been compelled by lack of means to surrender the practice of free treatment for those who are relatively poor, and payments are now being made by patients for their maintenance in hospitals according to the amount levied by the hospital almoner, who tries to take into account all the circumstances of each case. A small charge is made even for out-patients. They deal with 1,000,000 in-patients a year and 5,500,000 out-patients. These voluntary hospitals of late years have found it difficult to cope with the immense burden imposed upon them. Many patients who are in urgent need of medical or surgical relief cannot always obtain it, owing to the fact that the number of beds is insufficient. The hospitals have constantly to increase their accommodation both for the patients and for the nurses. The bigger the hospital and the more rapidly it increases in size, the greater is the difficulty in maintaining it. Hence the fear that has been expressed that before long the local authority or the State, or both, will have to come to the rescue. This may be warded off for the time being by the large donations of generous benefactors who fear that a request for public funds would mean public control, a withdrawal of contributions, and a weakening of the sense of individual responsibility. The income of the hospitals is £15,000,000 and £2,500,000 is derived from contributory associations, whose members pay 2d. or 3d. a week. Some of the voluntary hospitals are eking out their incomes by means of paying patients in private wards, for which a considerable charge is made. This is all to the good, provided that we do not forget that hospitals were originally designed to assist the poor. Today the growth of medical knowledge and medical research have made the hospital essential, because only there can be found the modern equipment and the expensive appliances which are required. In this sense the hospitals, with their 32 medical schools and 12,000 students, are becoming not less but more important every day.

A question for discussion in the near future is whether, if some control were exercised by a local authority, it would destroy the interest in these voluntary hospitals. I cannot quite accept the contention that our surgeons and our doctors would be unwilling to help and that the whole of the hospital work would become stereotyped, eliminating the human element. Public authorities do assist the provincial voluntary hospitals to the extent of about 8 per cent of the cost. However, we are not yet driven to face this question and meanwhile the hospitals of the local authorities are making things easier and relieving the strain of administering relief to large numbers of patients. In any case the treatment of infectious diseases and sanatorium treatment for tuberculosis is a matter for the local authorities, and now that the old Poor Law infirmaries have become hospitals and have been taken over by the health authorities, the whole standard of the municipal hospital has been raised. These institutions have been re-classified, re-equipped, and adapted for all modern requirements. It is true they have not always had the advantage of advice and assistance from the specialists of the voluntary hospitals, but that is becoming more common and they have enlisted the services of brilliant young men who accept the well-paid permanent posts at these hospitals which carry with them a pension later on in life. The only suggestion that we would venture to make, and that with some considerable hesitancy, is that a commission composed of doctors and surgeons, hygienists, architects, administrative officers and matrons or nurses, should be called together to consider the whole question of hospital treatment and administration. It would be, of course, an advisory commission and would have this value, that all the vast stores of knowledge which have been accumulated could be pooled, and, whether the hospital were voluntary or municipal, there is no doubt that valuable results would accrue.

When we consider the prevention of disease, and especially the first beginnings of disease, it is natural that we should regard as most important the work of the School Medical Officer. Medical inspection at schools, if under the control of a local authority, means that the scholars are inspected three times in the course of their elementary school life, at the ages of five, eight, and twelve. Thus there is always a chance of defects being detected in the early stages, and when these defects require further treatment, such as cannot be provided by the school nurse, they can be dealt with in hospitals or institutions where, after a further examination, they can be treated. Special schools are also provided for children suffering from certain defects found to be prevalent amongst the young. The school medical inspection has revealed ailments like epilepsy, mental deficiency, tuberculosis, rheumatism, heart disease, and disorders of the ear or eye which, unless they had been discovered in the early stages, would have had distressing results. Defective and decayed teeth, so common amongst school children, are a constant source of disease, and the number of children treated for dental trouble is amazing. The Reports of the Chief Medical Officer of the Board of Education, with all their encouragement, give an appalling account of the number of children who are suffering from defects, physical or mental, and medical inspection and treatment make it possible to eliminate to some extent the worst of these ailments and to give the child the chance of a healthy physical and mental life. As I am so rashly making suggestions, I would like to make one with regard to the improvement of the school medical service. It is that the examinations should be made more frequently and, if possible, once a year, since serious disorders may pass undetected during the three years that now elapse. Notwithstanding the utmost care taken by the doctor in his examination, he may fail to detect the disease in its early stage and in two years' time it may have so developed that it is difficult to apply a remedy. When we remember the heavy cost of providing for defective or diseased children, the argument that we should begin early and make our inspections continuous is surely conclusive.

An interesting experiment which may lead to much in the future is that of the Pioneer Health

Centre at Peckham. It possesses a first-rate swimming bath surrounded by a café, a gymnasium and other aids to physical health. It is a centralized service, the whole family being the unit. The father, the mother, and the children are all separately and regularly examined with a view to maintaining them in perfect health and to check the first beginnings of disease. Valuable research work is being carried out in this building by Dr. Scott Williamson, with the assistance of a grant from the Sir Halley Stewart Trust. This experiment it is hoped may be the forerunner of other similar institutions, and in time the local authority may take action along these lines, especially as so much stress is being laid on physical fitness.

The point, however, I wanted to emphasize is that we should begin early, that we should leave no gaps and that inspection should be as frequent as possible. If it were possible for the records of the child welfare clinics to be available to the school medical officer, and the records of the school medical officer be available to the public health authority, it would be something like the fulfilment of an ideal which preventive medicine has always advocated. Preventive medicine, if it is to be preventive, cannot be worked in watertight compartments. A good doctor, when he undertakes to treat a private patient, wants to know the history of that patient, and a specialist gets it from the general practitioner. In the same way there should be some record which can be consulted and there should be a "liaison" between all the different departments that deal with health or sickness.

Looking at the question from a still wider point of view, it has always to be remembered that health is positive and not negative. Our hygiene must therefore be creative and not merely curative. It does not mean merely the avoidance of disease, it means that physical and mental well-being are attained and maintained. There are many people who cannot be described as actually ill or diseased and yet at the same time they could hardly be regarded as healthy according to present physical standards. Preventive medicine means much more than the treatment of disease. Creative medicine means the building up of a robust healthy race. It means an improvement of the environment of the individual, just as the prevention of crime means much more than the treatment of misdemeanours. In fact, in dealing with the problem of health we have to remember the effect of proper housing, pure air, and good food, and we may add industrial hygiene and industrial psychology.[1] The appeal which is at present being made for more playing fields in this country on behalf of the King George Memorial Fund, will no doubt have a great influence on national health. Lack of physical training and exercise is one of the obstacles to health which we

[1] Since this was written the Government has appointed a committee to advise on the adminstration of the Physical Training and Recreation Act. A grant of £2,000,000 has been made in aid.

have to remove. Both Sweden and Germany are teaching us a lesson in this respect. The clearance of the slums will bring home to us the effect upon the health of the citizen of bad housing. Here, no doubt, we shall make great headway, and in five years' time all the worst slums in this country should have been replaced by decent houses and tenements. That is to say, a population something like 1,250,000 will have been placed in a much better environment. From the point of view of health the slum is one of our greatest dangers.

Housing is dealt with in a subsequent chapter, so there is no need to do more than mention the report issued last July on the Overcrowding Survey of England and Wales, which shows that 341,554 families are overcrowded according to the standard laid down by the Housing Act of 1935. These families are 3·8 per cent of the total working-class families in the country. Of the 9,000,000 houses inspected a further 380,000 families were only just above the overcrowding line, so that in this large number of families wherever a child passes the first or tenth birthday that family becomes overcrowded. Thus the slum population of 1,250,000 to which I have alluded as likely to be rehoused during this five years, should be regarded as at least two million persons, if we are to be on the safe side. Even in rehousing on new estates, if far away, there is a danger. A recent inquiry into the incidence of fatigue amongst workers in various trades showed that nothing was more fatiguing than the hours spent in overcrowded trains, buses and trams when travelling to and fro from work. It is a point to be borne in mind.

We have already dealt with the question of nutrition from the point of view of the child. We must carry it a step further. The Interim Report of the League of Nations Committee on the Problem of Nutrition makes this remark in its general survey: "In the light of modern knowledge it is abundantly clear that in no country does the whole population attain the standard scientifically desirable in the interests of health . . . defective nutrition is to be found among large sections of the population with the inevitable consequences of the prevalence of deficiency and the unsatisfactory standard of physique of the population as a whole. The high proportion of rejections on physical grounds of recruits for the army even in well-to-do countries is a typical illustration of a situation which prevails widely." The report then shows how in the United States a number of persons are insufficiently fed and a much larger number badly fed even in a period of great prosperity, and adds that economic depression made the position much worse. Sir John Orr, in his *Food, Health and Income*, it will be remembered, divided the population of the United Kingdom into three groups according to income. The average diet of the lowest income group, representing 10 per cent of the total population, is inadequate for perfect health in all of the constituents desired. The diet of the next group, representing 20 per cent of the population, is adequate only in total proteins and total fat. The third group, containing another 20 per cent and living at a better income level, has a diet adequate in energy value and protein and fat, but even the diet of this group is on the average below the standard in mineral and vitamin constituents. Accordingly it appears that, if we accept Sir John Orr's figures, the diet of at least 50 per cent of the population falls short of the desirable standard. To raise this half of the population to the level of a satisfactory dietary would require an increase of 16 per cent in milk consumption, 15 per cent in butter, 18 per cent in eggs, 12 per cent in meat, and 25 per cent increase of expenditure on fruit and vegetables. The diet would even then leave room for considerable improvement. In any case at least one-third are too poor to pay for Sir John Orr's adequate diet—the cost of which would be about 9s. per head for adults.

If, as seems to be the case, there is a close relationship between poverty and malnutrition, what steps can be taken to remove this great obstacle to national health, and is it by educational methods or by economic changes that we shall make the most rapid headway? If the latter, what should be the changes that we ought to effect? We all admit that an adequate standard of living is a *sine qua non* of social justice and peace. A hungry people is a dissatisfied and restless people. When we come to deal with methods for raising that standard we are up against economic and political problems that are not easy of solution. No doubt by education, by better organization, a good deal could be done to improve the health of the people, but the world-wide economic depression and the restrictions on the international movement of goods have made it almost inevitable that the poorest classes should suffer. What is required, however, is not only the cheapening of foodstuffs, but the availability of a regular supply at a regular price. It is the instability of prices which is such a hindrance to regular consumption and adequate nutrition. This limitation of food supplies, whatever may be the cause, does affect the question of national nutrition and therefore cannot be ignored. Malnutrition is only another name for ill-health and disease. The State can either quicken up the importation of these essential food products so that they may be sold at reasonable prices to the poorer population, or it can try to increase national production of certain of these foods, or, by public assistance, especially in the matter of distribution, it can enable such essential foods to be available to the poor at a cost within their means. Without dogmatizing as to methods we must abolish malnutrition by every means in our power if the population is to be maintained in health.

At a risk of "damnable iteration" let us once more emphasize the importance of co-ordinating the various services. Our National Health Insurance deals with some 18,000,000 contributors and costs £33,000,000 a year, one-third of which is paid by the Exchequer. We ought to try to bring together the medical services provided by local authorities and the medical services provided by the nation. Making full recognition of the work that has been done by the panel doctor and of the great advance that National Health Insurance implied, significant gaps in our health services still remain to be filled up. Even if our methods of dealing with the child and with young people were perfect (and they are far from perfect), there are still in all probability many millions of people who fail to have provision made for them in time of sickness, unless they are destitute or come under Public Assistance. Many of these people rely upon charitable aid in one form or another, since they are unable to defray the cost of proper medical attention. We do not forget the work that is being done by friendly societies and trade unions, but a very large number of those who are covered by this form of voluntary insurance only get help for sickness for a very short time in the shape of cash payments and, of course, no medical benefits are provided and the help of the general practitioner has to be called in. An estimate that has been given of the medical bill of Great Britain reaches the immense total of over £100,000,000 per annum, £13,000,000 being spent on medical benefits in connection with National Health Insurance, and £28,000,000 being the cost of public medical services falling on public funds.

Our future policy, then, with regard to the health problem, should be not to ignore the aspect which is purely medical but to lay stress upon the causes of ill-health, which have too often been ignored in the past. If we are to create a race of healthy citizens, we must create an environment which is likely to produce physical well-being, we must consider what are the causes of ill-health and how they can be remedied, and we must remember the immense loss that the nation suffers by reason of preventable disease and decreased efficiency in industry. There is a general dissatisfaction expressed on all sides with the hardships and sordid quality of life in our big towns, but this expression of sympathy and dissatisfaction is not directed definitely enough to the improvement both in the structure and the policy of our health services. Can we develop on community lines an administrative machine which, working through the agency of the local authorities and the State, will secure the building up of a comprehensive medical service available for all classes of the community? The present National Insurance scheme is not satisfactory. It can, of course, be enlarged and probably will be enlarged to include a much bigger group of insured persons with their families, but this may not be sufficient. At the same time, having proceeded along the lines of National Insurance, it is difficult to make the necessary changes. It would seem as though we had begun at the wrong end. We have laid too much stress on the idea of palliation instead of cure, but we certainly have not laid too much stress on explaining the causes of disease with a view to prevention. Research work is being pursued in all directions, but the research student is not over-paid and he often has to sacrifice a much more lucrative position in order to do that absolutely necessary work of exploration which is essential if we are to wipe out some of the worst enemies of mankind. Not less science but more science is needed, a new attitude towards the human body. It is a miracle of balanced forces. We upset the balance and then blame nature.

Can we look forward to a time when all our citizens will be normal as regards health? Socialized medicine has effected a great and unprecedented improvement. We are no doubt gradually dealing with our numerous bacteriological foes and perhaps, I ought to add, getting to know our bacteriological friends. The factors that make for health are being understood. We shun immortality with more intelligent forethought. Perhaps some day the problems of growth and of birth, which are largely chemical, will be solved. As the death rate is decreasing and the age limit expanding, there will come a time, we are told, supposing the birth rate continues to decrease, when England will consist of old or relatively old people. It will, however, be a long time before the average man and woman, much less the average young person, will be able to take advantage of the measures known to science which will preserve health and eliminate disease, unless, indeed, education improves beyond our present knowledge. There are still foolish people who insure their lives and then work themselves to death to pay the premiums. Doubtless education is proceeding and is being accelerated. The progress of man from the time when he gnawed his bone in some remote cave along the Mediterranean coast, or fought with the mammoth and the sabre-toothed tiger, has been continuous, and during the last hundred years rapid, but he still persists in believing that war is a necessity and, if he does not die of too much bombing from aeroplanes, he will no doubt lose his life by falling from an aeroplane. It is curious that after all these thousands of years, when we seem to a large extent to have conquered nature, that we cannot conquer this disposition to die before our time, that we cannot cure our physical and social ills. What is it in human beings that hinders so fundamental a development?

CHAPTER III

THE HOUSING OF THE CITIZEN

I am certain that I speak the truth, and a truth which can be confirmed by all experienced persons —clergy, medical men, and all who are conversant with the working class—that until their housing conditions are Christianized all hope of moral or social improvement is utterly in vain.

LORD SHAFTESBURY

CLEARLY linked with the question of health, whether of the child or the adult, is the problem of the proper housing of the people and especially of the working classes. During the last fifty years, a great change has come over the feeling of the nation with regard to this urgent problem. We have deliberately set ourselves to the work of rehousing our citizens. One of the many perplexities of the modern State is the unequal growth of the population and especially the population of the town. This question of the unequal distribution whether of people or of wealth, like the "black care" of the Roman poet, is always with us. We are constantly discovering that less than we want is more than we will ever have. The industrial revolution caused a rush to the town and the urban population increased at the expense of the country. This marked exodus from the country districts made it necessary both for the local authority and for the Government to take steps to counteract the centripetal force which attracted men to the city and incidentally compelled them to live in overcrowded conditions. The result was that large towns became unwieldy. The original cottages and tenement houses inhabited by a forgotten people were allowed to remain and became derelict, while new houses and cottages, built at a time when housing regulations and by-laws were almost unknown, were erected 40 or 50 to the acre with inadequate air space, insufficient sanitary accommodation, and in many cases were shoddily constructed. In fact you hardly dared take down the scaffolding until the walls had been papered.

Not so the houses of the middle classes or the rich. The real problem is, of course, the housing of the working classes, the millions of people who cannot do without shelter even if the rent which they pay is far too great a drain upon their weekly earnings. It is unfortunate that, as a result of the factory system and the introduction of machinery, no sufficient effort was made to assimilate the populations that poured into the urban areas. There was no planned attempt to supply proper housing accommodation and the result was that the worst forms of jerry-building were pardoned or condoned because of the necessity for more houses. This housing problem has not been seriously dealt with until the last two decades. It will explain many of the evils which have sprung from insanitary accommodation, evils that are cumulative and doubtless account for much of the disease and the ill-health that our medical officers are trying to overcome.

We may say that the growth of the town is the note of the century. A hundred years ago two-thirds of the people lived in the country; today more than two-thirds live in the towns. Sir Arthur Helps once wrote an essay which he called *Towns may be too large*. He wrote at a time when towns had not reached the magnitude of the present day. Take London, for example, this huge leviathan which we have made. It is becoming increasingly impossible to get from the centre of the town into the country without a considerable journey by rail or bus. Long lines of unlovely streets are growing up around London, stretching far out into the green belt which (Heaven be praised!) is being saved in part by the efforts of the London County Council and the surrounding county authorities. We are only just in time to prevent Greater London becoming a huge conglomeration of nondescript houses some twenty-five miles across, whether from north to south or east to west.

Since the housing problem is the heritage of many generations, it is becoming increasingly important that the determined attempt now being made to re-house slum dwellers in healthy homes should be supported by every thoughtful citizen. While hundreds of thousands of people live in slum conditions in basement dwellings, or tumbledown tenements, we must not rest on our oars and the more so because we are pulling against the tide. The town is still growing, although the centre of the big city may be losing some of its population. I do not believe in being too doctrinaire about housing in flats or cottages. We have to adapt ourselves to the conditions which we find in existence. It is still the case that, while we have factories in the town and while it is essential that many workers should reach their work in the early hours of the morning, you cannot compel them to live on the outskirts of the big city at the cost of several shillings a week for transport and the prospect of a very early start in the morning. For these people we must pursue the policy of London, Liverpool, Birmingham, Manchester, and other large cities, erecting flats in the centre of the town for those who are compelled to live near their work and building on new estates outside the town from which speedy transport is possible at not too high a cost. In this connection we have to remember that there is a growing tendency to remove the factory from the centre of the city to the outskirts or even to the country beyond, and this naturally makes all the difference to the planning of the new estates near such factories. The houses in close proximity to these factories are speedily occupied and a somewhat higher rent can be obtained than would otherwise be the case.

In a dim kind of way we have at last come to

understand that you can no more leave the growth of a town to chance than you can the growth of a child. We demand a more orderly conception of civic life, more responsibility and more foresight on the part of the municipality and a large outlook on the part of the Government. For this reason, although the Housing and Town Planning Acts are not entirely satisfactory, they have to be commended because they were the first step towards the setting up of a standard of housing approximating to our ideal. I use the word "approximating" because undoubtedly the ideal is not spasmodic or sporadic housing, but the satellite town linked to the larger centre yet containing within itself the possibility of civic and municipal life.

If there is one problem more than another which requires planning and control it is the housing problem, employing as it does 850,000 men. The haphazard construction of houses by the speculating builder, to supply a certain definite demand, may or may not be a success. It is open to doubt; but considering the importance we now attach to environment, the question is worth far closer study in order that the new estates shall conform to a high standard of building and should have in connection with them all those amenities of open space, light, and air which we are just beginning to regard as necessary. I admit that even the haphazard construction of houses is better than the overcrowding in the slums so dangerous to health and so subversive of moral restraint. This crowding together is one of the somewhat nebulous gains of modern civilization, and it is much to be deplored that so many of the working classes seem to take pleasure in noisy and congested surroundings. The smoky town affects them with a queer kind of nostalgia. They like the glare and the activity of many people; the country they find to be dull and gloomy. It is our fault and not theirs. They have not perhaps sufficient resources in themselves and need to be brightened up by external surroundings. Sordid houses make sordid people.

This is not the place to deal with rural housing or enter upon any discussion of the Housing and Town Planning Act, nor need we do more than mention the Housing of the Working Classes Act, which enabled local authorities to purchase land and to set the pace for the construction of working-class estates. Our object is rather to concentrate upon slum clearance and the new Overcrowding Act. Under the Housing Act of 1935 there are specific provisions for the abatement and prevention of overcrowding. The general idea is to provide a standard for measuring overcrowding and, subject to suitable safeguards, to make it a public offence to infringe that standard. Broadly speaking that standard is the separation of the sexes at night, not more than two persons to one room, three to two rooms, five to three rooms, etc. Children under ten count only as half a person and babies under one year are ignored altogether. The standard room must contain 90 square feet, say about ten feet by nine, and if it is actually larger than this it counts as one and a half or two rooms.

With these facts in our minds we are able to examine the survey undertaken by local authorities in pursuance of their duty under the Act to which I have referred. It is styled the Prevention and Abatement of Overcrowding section. The survey has now been accomplished and the Report was published in July of last year. That Report shows that nearly 9,000,000 dwellings were inspected, equal to the total number of houses existing in 1931. The survey shows that, taking the standard laid down by the Housing Act, 341,554 families were overcrowded, that is to say, 3·8 per cent of the total of the working-class families in the country. These families were badly overcrowded. The Report goes on to state that a further 380,000 families were only just above the official line; for example, whenever a child passes its first or its tenth birthday in one of the 380,000 families, technically the house becomes overcrowded. Over 43 per cent of the overcrowded families are shown to have at least 80 per cent of the minimum accommodation required and only 4·8 per cent have less than half the minimum accommodation required. About 46 per cent of all the working-class families in the country are so well housed that the number of persons in each family could be doubled and yet overcrowding as defined would not ensue. We are told that 30·4 per cent of all overcrowded families consisted of small families up to four units in size, while 27·7 per cent of all overcrowded families consisted of large families of seven units or over. Another important point which people are apt to forget when they look at the statistics, is that over 43 per cent of the overcrowded dwellings were one or two rooms and only 2·7 per cent had five rooms or more. *The average overcrowded dwelling is therefore, according to the figures given,* 37 *per cent smaller than the average uncrowded dwelling, though it is inhabited by a family* 74 *per cent larger.* The result of the survey generally, then, seems to show that a very large number are overcrowded and a still larger number are on the border line and likely to be overcrowded at any time. The worst overcrowding, as we would expect, is in the East End of London and the North-East Coast. Shoreditch and Stepney are the most overcrowded of the London boroughs. Sunderland is the worst overcrowded of all the large cities.

There is, as a result of the new building, a centrifugal movement of population, and I see that the official figures published by the London County Council show that, since the last Census 1931, 150,000 Londoners have left the County of London and are now housed a few miles outside in estates like Becontree, Morden, Norbury, and White Hart Lane in Tottenham. This migration has eased the problem of housing Londoners, but there still remains the difficulty of housing the very large numbers who are overcrowded and must at the same time remain in London because of their occupation. We still have in one square mile of Shoreditch over 90,000 people, and it is typical of many working-class districts. St. Pancras and Paddington until recently were very little better so far as overcrowding is concerned. St. Pancras has improved owing to the construction of flats, but if we take the figures for St. Pancras and Paddington, 60 per cent of the families are living three or more in a house intended for one family. In Islington and Finsbury the corresponding figures are 50 per cent, in Shoreditch, Southwark, Kensington, Marylebone, and Holborn 40 per cent. In Finsbury 60 per cent of all the families are living in one or two rooms.

The general effect of all the movement of population during the last ten years is that the artisan population are now better housed. They have a larger choice of housing and their families are smaller. The poorer people until recently tended to crowd together more than ever, and it is to relieve the pressure on this section of the population that the new legislation is largely devised. For the first time statutory priority will be given to tenants who most need new and cheap houses.

The question of slum clearance which naturally follows from the overcrowding survey, although it is only one of a mass of postponed problems, is perhaps the most important. An overcrowded house is, of course, not necessarily a slum, and the local authorities instructed to proceed with their campaign against slums have made estimates of the numbers of houses that require to be declared for clearance purposes. A clearance area is a district that contains dwellings in a thoroughly bad state of repair or are so congested as to be dangerous to public health. These areas consist almost entirely of worn-out, verminous dwellings closely packed together. They have to be demolished and the area cleared. A clearance area may belong to a local authority or to private individuals, but the local authority has the power to include in a clearance area huts, or tents, or caravans, or any fixed structure which is used as a permanent dwelling and is unfit for human habitation. The new Act allows dwelling-houses to be excluded from the clearance order if they are only in the area owing to their bad arrangement in relation to other buildings. When a slum area is compulsorily acquired, if compensation for the site value had been settled on the basis of the 1919 Act, the owner can claim to have the matter reopened and the local authority may also compensate any owner of a house which, though unfit for human habitation, has been fairly well maintained in all the circumstances. Shopkeepers in insanitary houses in a clearance scheme may also be compensated by reason of the disturbance of trade or business. The Government is prepared to subsidize these clearance schemes to the extent of £1,000,000, and so far as can be ascertained the Act will require the demolition and replacing of 250,000 houses in five years. The replacement can be effected either by the local authority, with the help of Government loans at a low rate of interest ($3\frac{3}{4}$ per cent for sixty years including sinking fund), or by the local authority with the help of the building societies. On the average it is expected that every year slum clearance will be carried out to such an extent as will equal all the slum clearance that has been accomplished in the sixty years up to 1932. The housing of the dispossessed slum dwellers will naturally be effected either by erecting five- to eight-storey tenements in the big towns, in which case the cost of sites is very heavy and the rents of the flats proportionately higher, or the rehousing is planned to take place on new estates outside the town, and of these new estates there are many illustrations not only near London but near all the large provincial city centres. Outside London the rents payable for three rooms by the tenants average between 5s. and 7s. 6d. a week after allowing for the effect of the subsidy.

A great difficulty that the London County Council has had to contend with is that of finding suitable sites for these new tenements, and the Hackney Marshes controversy, so happily solved, is still in our minds in that connection. Whether the problem is to rehouse the slum dweller or to satisfy the normal housing demand in London as houses are pulled down, it is always a difficult and costly undertaking which the London County Council has faced with great courage. On March 31st of last year the London County Council had provided 72,979 dwellings and of these 17,934 are flats in block dwellings; the lowest inclusive rent for two rooms is 4s. 6d.; for five rooms 13s. 1d. In the district of St. Pancras alone, we have the Ossulton Street flats, housing thousands of families, built by the London County Council, the flats of the St. Pancras Borough Council, opened by Princess Mary, and also the flats erected by the St. Pancras Housing Improvement Society. Under the 1930 Act the London County Council has embarked on a Slum Clearance Scheme which will cost £35,000,000 and involves the displacement from slum areas of 250,000 people: about 12,000 people were rehoused during the year ending March 31, 1936. The largest clearance scheme planned is 46 acres in the northern part of Bethnal Green, the cost being £1,750,000, the number of people dispossessed being 5,741.

Although nearly 2,000,000 new houses were built in Great Britain between 1919 and 1930, about half being erected by private enterprise, only spasmodic efforts had been made to clear the slums, but now since 1931, under the National Government, more than 1,000,000 houses have been built and already 420,000 occupiers of insanitary houses have been rehoused in well-built homes, and we are still rehousing at the rate of over 200,000 persons a year. It is now not so much fresh housing legislation that is required as determined and steady progress in this work of slum clearance and rehousing the dispossessed.

We have indicated our view that the building of lofty tenements is not ideal though the only solution for certain types of manual workers. The best solution, wherever it is possible, is to build a new estate outside the towns. We have many illustrations, some of them good and some of them bad. I think we may lay down certain propositions in regard to these new estates which will probably not be gainsaid. In the first instance they must be planned so as to preserve the countryside around the town and to leave a broad agricultural belt which could, if required, be used for playing fields and open spaces. Secondly, they should be carefully planned, taking on the aspect of garden suburbs and preserving the amenities of the countryside wherever possible. Thirdly, it is probably unwise to build merely one class of house on these estates; it must be a mistake to segregate classes of society, and the best illustrations are those in which provision is made for any class of house with rents of 7s. or 10s. a week upwards. There are many estates in which this is possible, because the working-class houses have been well planned and well built and, situated in these surroundings, are not an eyesore. Finally, there is no doubt whatever that the management of these estates is not only a problem of housing accommodation: it is a question of wise, firm, and sympathetic management. Perhaps one ought to add that no large new estate should be planned without having full regard to educational facilities for the children, and for some central meeting place in order that the residents may gradually build up a civic life.

The London County Council, of course, has taken the lead in developing these new estates, although they are a little apt to lose sight of the sense of responsibility when the location is outside the London County Council area. At least twelve estates have been provided for people who have to live in the outer areas. The number of houses constructed is 60,000 and the largest estate is Becontree. Becontree is sometimes confused with Dagenham because the estate was originally known as Dagenham and built near Dagenham village, but recently the railway station, once called Dagenham, has been re-christened Becontree. One of the unfortunate confusions is that of local government areas, for the estate is in three local government areas, Ilford, Barking, and Dagenham. Dagenham is known to us because Ford's new works are situated in the Dagenham Urban District. The population of the whole town is about 120,000, and considering the rapidity with which it has been developed, there is perhaps some excuse for the fact that the London County Council, although it provided gas, water, electricity, and sewerage, did not perhaps sufficiently take into account the necessity for assisting public and voluntary social services. I understand that this omission is being remedied. It is not wholly working class, although the various housing acts under which the London County Council built do provide houses for working-class people at rents which they can afford to pay; but it is doubtful whether there are many former occupants of slum areas living in this district, since it is quite likely that the transport charges in this case are too heavy. They probably came from overcrowded boroughs. It ought to be remembered that the people who live in Becontree were not compelled to live there by the London County Council as the result of demolition. For the most part they came there in order to get better conditions, or to live near the Ford works, employing many thousands of people. The lowest inclusive rent for a four-roomed (non-parlour) cottage would be 10s. 5d. and the highest for the same number of rooms is 23s. 4d.

If we go to the provinces we find that Birmingham is building 13,000 houses on twenty estates, Bristol over 12,000 on nine estates, the largest being Bedminster. Manchester has built or is building 40,000 houses on fifteen estates: the largest of these is at Wythenshawe in Cheshire, which after a long struggle Manchester was able to secure, although it was outside their area at the time. Wythenshawe alone, when fully built up, will have 26,000 houses.

Sheffield's programme is 9,000 houses on nine estates, to rehouse slum dwellers, the largest being the Manor Estate with a population of 3,800. Bedford, Chesterfield, and Edinburgh are also building on estates, and the tendency is all in this direction. The subsidies originally granted and now pooled for slum clearance, will enable the slum dwellers to be rehoused by grants which will reduce the rents. Thus a cottage on a new estate with three bedrooms and no parlour can be built for a little over £300 and can be let at about 10s. a week, whereas we should have to add, in London at all events, at least another 2s. a week for the rent of a three-roomed flat.

One great advantage of building on the outskirts of the town is that land is cheaper, that a garden is possible and almost universal, and the only drawback is the cost of transport to the town, which may be anything from 2s. 6d. to 5s. a week. Leeds is trying to re-house 111,000 people on new estates, and this is in addition to the building in the centre of the town on sites at one time occupied by back-to-back houses, of which some 30,000 are being cleared away. On these town sites they are building about 1,000 tenement flats. Next to the London County Council this is the largest housing scheme of any city and it is estimated that it will cost some millions of pounds, although we may anticipate that the rateable value of the city will be greatly increased.

We have mentioned Manchester, which is clearing

15,000 slum dwellings, and as an important part of their housing programme not connected with slum clearance, has created a new garden suburb at Wythenshawe. Already 6,000 houses have been erected out of the total of 26,000. The estate consists of 5,500 acres, and about half of it will be left for open spaces or used for agricultural purposes. Wythenshawe is an illustration of what ought to be done. Practically the only way by which Manchester could develop new estates on right lines was to go south, and after a long fight, both in the city council and in Parliament, they were able to secure for the purpose of this estate Tatton Park in Cheshire and the surrounding land, which was in every respect suitable for their purpose. Wythenshawe is planned when finished to house 100,000 people, and it is important to note that these people are not to be all of one class, although some of the residents will be middle class or well to do. The plan includes space for a considerable number of factories and the houses which these factory workers will occupy are to be let at low rents; but the important thing to remember is that every attempt is being made to secure that the houses shall be of good quality and artistic in appearance. About 1,000 acres will constitute the agricultural belt and serve also the purpose of open spaces and playing fields. Another 100 acres is being reserved for a golf course, and the park of the Tatton family, consisting of 250 acres, is to be a permanent open space. The planning is ideal. There are two broad main roads with subsidiary roads giving access to the houses, so that children and tradesmen need not appear on the main roads except for short distances. The main roads have wide margins with grass, trees, and beds of flowers, and the houses are separated from the street by 150 feet of open space. Manchester has reserved 3,000 acres for housing and the plans show a minimum of four houses to the acre and a maximum of twelve. Two new schools have already been erected for the children of the residents, largely on the open-air principle, from 5–10 acres being allotted to each school. I ought to add that Sir E. D. Simon, a former Lord Mayor of Manchester, has been a moving spirit in this great new estate experiment, and it is to him very largely that its success up to the present is due.

It is hardly necessary to mention the work that has been done by the pioneer efforts of individual employers like Cadbury at Bournville, Rowntree at Earswick, and Lever at Port Sunlight. All three are too well known to need any description. Letchworth, the outcome of Mr. Ebenezer Howard's book *Garden Cities of Tomorrow*, was the first garden city to be established. It is interesting because it represents a self-contained municipality, not dependent upon the outer world except in so far as many of its inhabitants come to London every day to engage in various occupations. Another illustration is that of Welwyn Garden City, which is also a more or less self-contained centre. In this case also many of the people come to London daily. Both in the case of Letchworth and of Welwyn Garden City the real effect has been to give a middle-class population a better house at a lower rent. Both are town-planning experiments on a large scale. The ideal of both was to associate with the town both industrial work and agricultural, so that the movement from the country to the town might be stayed.

There has been a great deal of criticism, much of it unjust, with regard to the Government's attempt to solve the housing problem and especially in respect of slum clearance. The main responsibility rests with the local authorities, although public utility societies and private enterprise will play their part. It was thought that the local authorities, while dealing with slum clearance, would not be inclined to build houses to let to the poorest classes at rents which they can afford to pay; but this assumption that the local authorities are not interested in the welfare of their poorest citizens is not justified by facts. So much interest has been created in the housing problem that even reluctant local authorities have been stimulated into effective action. It may be true that all the slums in our large towns cannot be cleared in five years, yet judging from the advance that has already been made all the worst slums will have been dealt with during that period, and a large part of the rehousing schemes will have been carried out. I do not anticipate any great confusion or conflict arising between the local authority and the public utility societies. There is room for the work of both, and the larger the problem the more likely it is that the local authority will plan a rational and a complete scheme. Of course there is a danger that there may be unco-ordinated clearance, haphazard reconditioning, and piece-meal and unregulated development in certain areas, but for the most part the authorities are now convinced of the danger of creating new slums and of rehousing as speedily as possible those who are dispossessed. It would have been an advantage if there had been some one controlling and co-ordinating authority, directing the whole of the housing campaign. That also would have implied legislation, for we can hardly expect the local authorities to accept the guidance of a housing board unless that board were backed by legislation.

There is one danger which we foresee and that is the lack of management of these huge new blocks of buildings and of new estates. We expect too much of human nature if we imagine that people who have been living in slums all their lives and are creatures of their environment, and perhaps inured to unhygienic surroundings, will immediately adopt the new standard which the new house will set. Nothing but firm and kindly management will solve that problem, otherwise we are out for disillusionment, but that in the great majority of cases the slum dweller can be adapted to his new conditions I have no doubt whatever. It is a pity, of course, that Greater London, with its 125 different local authorities concerned with housing, could not have been treated as a unity. The London County Council alone, which is supposed to co-ordinate the 28 municipal boroughs, has to encounter a great deal of delay and loss of efficiency.

The method adopted of granting a subsidy towards the cost of new houses required to rehouse former slum tenants or to abate overcrowding is practically the method adopted in all the Housing Acts since the war with this exception. An Exchequer contribution is made towards the building of blocks of flats of not less than three storeys high on sites that are expensive. Such, for example, we find in London. The contribution will increase with the cost of the site including the cost of development. If, for example, the cost of the developed site is from £1,500 to £4,000 an acre, the subsidy for forty years is £6 a year per flat. From £4,000 an acre it goes up by £1 a year per flat, until the cost reaches £8,000 an acre, when the subsidy is £9 a year per flat. After that it is £1 a year per flat for every £2,000 or part of £2,000 increase. The Act takes it for granted that it is impossible to build in the centre of a large town without some help from the Government if the rents are to be such as the working classes can pay. The estimate that the Government makes is that the average subsidy for each new flat will be £10 a year for forty years.

There can be no doubt that the life of these well-built tenements will be not less than a hundred years. Since the whole problem is how much the working classes can afford to pay out of their weekly wage, and especially the weekly wage of the unskilled labourer, it is worth while considering whether anything could be done to give special assistance. It is just possible that there may have to be some modification of the rates or perhaps a measure of de-rating in the case of the poorer section of the population, or a measure of rent rebates according to size of income and the family. If we look at the special areas we shall see that the rates tend to be very high, and very low in areas that are prosperous. The poorer people, therefore, in many cases live in areas where the rates and rents combined make it difficult for the family to live and the natural tendency is therefore to overcrowding. On the other hand, these working-class areas have a low rateable value and the burden of the social services is also very heavy. The simpler method, therefore, is a direct subsidy, since the de-rating of working-class houses is hardly feasible without a general reform of local government.

There has been a good deal of criticism of the payment of compensation for houses in clearance areas that have been well maintained or as well maintained as was possible under the circumstances. At first these landlords were not compensated, but it was regarded as rather a hardship that comparatively poor people (although not necessarily poor) who had expended money on trying to keep up the standard of the house should receive no compensation. What has happened is that the Government decision was taken as a result of hard cases brought to their notice. If it had been merely a matter of vested interests perhaps the Government would not have given way, but many cases were brought to light of people with very small incomes who own some property in an area that ought to be cleared and in these cases their property was notably, as regards condition, much better than the surrounding property—that is to say, their houses were in a state of habitable repair. Some people have contended that it should be left to private enterprises to build the new houses, but surely the local authority is the right agency under the circumstances. It is responsible for the maintenance of the roads, the lighting of the streets, the sewerage and the drainage, and by the Act responsible for declaring whether the houses should be cleared or allowed to remain. They are in every way responsible for the health of the community and it is therefore far better that the local authority should have the responsibility of supplying the need for new working-class houses. Whether the Housing Advisory Committee, consisting for the most part of experts, will be of great value in so far as central planning is concerned it is too soon to say, but there is no reason why their recommendations should not be adopted either by the local authority or by public utility societies. Under the Act the local authorities have power to transfer their responsibilities to housing management committees, but the proposed transfer of power is optional and it is not likely that many local authorities will consent to abdicate their functions in this manner. Indeed, where they do so abdicate we might give up almost all hope of proper provision being made for the amenities of social life, public gardens, and playing fields, schools, libraries, and public baths, etc., all of which amenities mean a charge on the local rates. You can hardly expect any local authority to allow an independent body of people to impose new rates on the citizens of the town.

Meanwhile a great deal is being made of the importance of building one hundred satellite towns of 50,000 each as the only policy worthy of commendation. I am afraid it is an impossible project, unless you are asking for a housing and social welfare dictator who would incidentally have power to reorganize all the industries of the country. It sounds like stealing a march on the millennium.

The estimated Exchequer contribution for 1934 to 1935 building is £16,000,000, and for 1935 to 1936 it is £16,250,000. Of all the houses built since the war two-thirds were built by local authorities and one-third by private enterprise. The capital cost of these houses is estimated at £671,000,000, so that it can hardly be said in fairness that the problem has been utterly neglected. It is thought that by 1950 nearly 2,000,000 more houses will be wanted, but it is too early yet to prophesy the effect of the decrease in population. The most urgent question is to clear away the slums and rehouse those who are in immediate need.

In surveying the whole problem we have to remember, first of all, that we must have a sufficiency of houses to abate overcrowding; secondly, that all slums must be cleared and the population rehoused under satisfactory conditions either in flats or cottages; thirdly, that so far as possible the environment should be good, that is to say, in the town there should be space for gardens or grass which can be used by the inhabitants. In the case of the new estates there should be large gardens, and the planning should be such as would give the best results as regards sunshine and fresh air. It is true that many of the cottages that are being built for the working classes are not well built, but in the main they are a great improvement on their predecessors, and the probability is that they will last a couple of generations at least, so that it is to be hoped that while we are building we will try to make them as permanent as possible, taking into account the cost and the necessity for low rents. We now all admit that the housing problem is not an isolated problem but bound up with all other social questions, like poverty and unemployment. We are facing it full of hope because we believe that in less than a generation there will be no slums, unless perchance we create new ones, and because we feel sure that the abolition of the slum and the rehousing of the poor will not only improve the health and well-being of the people but will make possible a great advance from the intellectual and moral point of view.

CHAPTER IV

THE SECURITY OF THE CITIZEN

A characteristic of the new national machinery, fully apparent towards the end of Queen Victoria's reign, was the close inter-relation that had grown up on the one hand between private philanthropic effect and State control, and on the other between local and central government. . . . Voluntary and private effort, aided by the State, did many things that in other countries of Europe were done solely by the State or were not done at all.

G. M. TREVELYAN

IN the preface to *Androcles and the Lion* Mr. Bernard Shaw makes this remark: "Until the community is organized in such a way that the fear of bodily want is forgotten as completely as the fear of wolves already is in civilized capitals, we shall never have a decent social life." With that statement, I imagine, we are all agreed, but the problem is not so much how to get agreement in theory as to how to obtain it in practice. There was published some years ago a book by an Austrian named Wittels. It is called *An End of Poverty*. He takes no great credit for the ideas it contains, but attributes them rather to Josef Popper, who was nicknamed Lynceus because of his keen insight. In this book he sketches a proposal for transforming the nation into a universal civil service, each member receiving for the services rendered over a term of years a standard minimum of food, shelter, and clothing. After subsistence had been provided a certain cultural minimum would also be supplied. Anything beyond the subsistence and cultural minima would be accounted luxury. The economic system of today based on private ownership would continue. It sounds Utopian, but generations of progress have seen the achievement of many ideals that we once regarded as fantastic. It may be that with the growth of education and the increase of goodwill even poverty itself may be regarded as anomalous.

Perhaps there is nothing that the individual citizen desires more than security in life, security as regards his shelter, his food, his clothing, and his old age, yet we are constantly hearing today of the indifference of the young of this generation as regards the future. We are told that a wave of recklessness has swept over the country, that men and women are quite indifferent about the desirability of saving for old age or a rainy day, that there is a growing desire to have luxuries on the instalment plan, and that this in itself is a sign of the degeneration which is setting in. It is argued that the State has gradually undermined the independence of the people, that Health Insurance, Unemployment Insurance, and Old Age Pensions, and now the Unemployed Assistance Board have rendered it unnecessary for them to save and that consequently they just pursue the line of least resistance and spend all that they receive from day to day. There is, of course, a modicum of truth in a rather sweeping condemnation of present-day youth, but in view of the enormous increase in savings it cannot be the whole truth and there is not much doubt that, given the opportunity, the great mass of people in this country desire security and would take the necessary steps to obtain it if they felt there was any chance of accomplishing their purpose. That many do save for a rainy day is shown by the fact that the volume of small savings in this country amounts to £2,400,000,000, or an average of £200 per family. Even if we say that the larger part of this represents middle-class savings, there is still a very large sum included in the assets of friendly societies, the Co-operative movement, and the trade unions, not to speak of the Post Office Savings Bank. It does not mean, of course, that these savings are available at a moment's notice, but I mention the figures because they do disprove the contention that the majority of our working classes are reckless and disinclined to save.

The present social order is based on individualism and has been for hundreds of years, but there has been a considerable growth in what we may call social idealism. We demand a higher standard of life, of health, of education, of housing. We have demanded and we have obtained better conditions for labour, although these conditions are still far from being perfect. Collectivism in various forms has diminished the risks of life and taxation, which implies also redistribution of wealth, has diminished poverty and increased opportunity. The economic depression which descended upon us in 1928 dealt a shattering blow to our *laissez-faire* complaisance. In common with countries all over the world, Great Britain suffered, although perhaps not quite to the same extent. As a result of the unsettlement due to economic pressure, democratic government disappeared first in one country and then another. We have witnessed a wave of economic nationalism throughout the world, and it has not left Great Britain untouched. In many countries there has been a rapid growth of unemployment and even in England, which has fared so much better than most, there has been a huge waste of life, at any rate as regards quality. A million people have become accustomed to a sense of dependence and have suffered in morale as a result of enforced idleness. We are conscious that hundreds of thousands of these unemployed will never again become useful citizens. The iron has eaten into their souls and they feel bitterly that they are suffering a great national injustice.

The movement is not altogether static. This depression in trade is also dynamic in its effects. The way in which work and workers have migrated within the last few months from the north to the south, the substitution of women and young people for the adult, regional changes on the part of wage seekers throughout the community, all these are indications of the fluctuations which are constantly taking place and which imply for a certain portion of the population insecurity. We need never fear a violent revolution in this country if the working classes are well paid, well housed, and have a certainty of a contented old age. But these things are an ideal and not a practical reality, although no nation in the whole world has done more than Great Britain to cope with the problems that have been set up by the world crisis. This crisis has challenged the idealism of the twentieth century, and there has sprung up an ineradicable sense of social responsibility. We no longer regard social insurance as merely supplementing the wage system. We now have to care for and maintain a large army of able-bodied citizens of all ages and of all kinds. Unemployment is not a small or personal problem. When more than thirty years ago I wrote a little book on "Unemployment, a National Question," many people regarded unemployment as a purely individual matter. It was a harsh and anti-social attitude regarding the workless. We now know that to a large extent unemployment is a symptom of economic fluctuations and due to national disequilibrium. It is also an international as well as a national question. No doubt, to some extent, it is a question of personal quality or adaptability, but there remains a residuum of unemployment of vast size which needs to be socialized. This, at the moment, is being dealt with by insurance, public assistance, and voluntary aid. Throughout the world this difficulty of adjusting our institutions so as to enable them to deal with this problem of unemployment still remains. The United States is confronted today with the necessity of insuring unemployed millions, but she hesitates to interfere with a free and unregulated labour market by applying a plan of State insurance to the labour battalions who are unfortunately in the position of compulsory idleness. Unemployment insurance, as we have it in England, is just a form of enforced thrift aided by a State subsidy. It is given without a test of means or needs. It is given as a right and not as a poverty payment, and for the large number who run the risk of descending to the poverty line there is irrefragable proof of its great value.

There are 13,000,000 workers insured under the main scheme and 700,000 agricultural labourers have also become insurable under a special provision for agriculture. Leaving out domestic servants, who are not yet insured, nearly all who are employed in industry and commerce, if they are earning not more than £250 a year, are now insurable. It is not improbable that later on the scope of the insurance scheme may be extended up to incomes of £400 per annum. There is a fixed scale of benefits payable for six months to all who have satisfied contribution conditions. In cases where there is a comparatively good contribution record the benefits may be extended to twelve months. More than half the unemployed are at present receiving either benefits or allowances.

When the benefits are exhausted the unemployed may apply for assistance to the Unemployed Assistance Board. Allowances are made after inquiry according to the need of the household concerned. About 45 per cent of all the unemployed receive these allowances and it is important to note that more than half of these would be in the Special Areas. The Unemployment Act of 1934 was a successful attempt to set the Unemployment Fund on a sound basis. Previous to that Act workers with a good contribution record were really helping to support the chronically unemployed, and the Treasury still regards the huge debt of £115,000,000 as being repayable by the Fund at the rate of £5,000,000 a year. This is a good bargain from the Treasury point of view, but somewhat unfair to the employer and the employed. However, increased contributions, improved trade, and limited liability have made a surplus possible and this surplus is growing. So much is this the case that Sir William Beveridge's Statutory Committee recommended the reduction by 1d. a week of all contributions, and accordingly the amount was reduced from 10d. to 9d. in 1936. This reduction meant that the State, the employer, and the worker, all three benefited to the extent of about £2,250,000 a year. Notwithstanding this recent reduction the accumulated reserve is growing and it is estimated that the disposable surplus is now over £30,000,000. Of course, much depends upon the rate of unemployment falling and not rising. If the rate of unemployment should fall, say, to 12 per cent, there is every prospect of a large surplus. We are witnessing within our borders something like a trade boom which may last and probably will last for another two years. If meanwhile there should be any real lightening of the international situation, it will be followed by a period of world prosperity, in which case the Government would benefit to a still larger extent.

No doubt insurance might break down under the great strain if world depression again seriously affected this country. and assistance by the Unemployment Assistance Board in this case would have to be given to greatly increased numbers. There will always be some resentment felt in the case of any inquiry into the means of people who have to seek such assistance. Labour resents the adjustment of relief according to resources. If need is to be taken into account it seems difficult to believe that the means test can be totally abolished. The formula is "needs minus available resources." This formula has gained the consent of all except the Labour opposition which, in objecting to any means test, have perhaps failed to see that the 13,000,000 insured wage earners might be averse to a policy by which these grants were made to people who have not contributed—grants, moreover, of equal amount to people of unequal incomes. It seems certain that such a policy would fail. Surely the line to take is to raise the standard of needs and then the means test will only operate in extreme cases.

The amended benefits in connection with the Assistance Board have now come into force. They affect 620,000 people who at the present moment are costing £38,000,000. In future the annual cost will be £38,750,000. The new regulations do away with a good many anomalies and allow for a redistribution of existing benefits on lines which are more flexible and more just. They replace the regulations which came into force in January 1935, and then were temporarily withdrawn owing to criticism. Increased allowances will be made to probably 200,000 existing applicants and there may be and probably will be a reduction in payment in about 10 per cent of the cases. There has been a revision of rent allowances and of deductions for earnings of members of the family of unemployed workers and much wider powers have been given to appeal tribunals and local advisory committees. The new regulations are elastic. There is no uniform basis, but allowances are adjustable in the light of local factors. To meet all the possible exceptional cases, and nearly every case is exceptional, the 150 advisory committees, representative but nonelective, will have a determining voice. But even from their decisions there is an appeal to one of the 138 appeal tribunals.

The primary concern of these new regulations is to provide for the wants of households and individuals without resources bringing them above the level of want. There is little doubt that the cumulative effect of the changes will relieve the distress where it would be most acute. The final test must be, does it effectively supply their needs? The Labour argument is that these men, being unemployed not of their own volition, and being persons who have exhausted their insurance benefit, are entitled to as much without a means test as any unemployed still in benefit. It is difficult to justify this, and it is quite possible, as I have said, that even the unemployed themselves who make a contribution would regard this equality of treatment as unfair. There is no doubt that relief without need would put a premium on idleness, and the only question remains as to whether these non-needy cases can be eliminated or whether the Labour Party would insist on their being included.

To remove the sense of injustice resulting from harsh decisions the Government will be compelled to trust more and more to a flexible, discreet, and judicious local administration. For this work well-paid, well-educated, and sympathetic administrators are required, and here perhaps we touch one of the weaknesses of public administration today. In any case it is quite certain that you can easily overdo the idea of centralization and local institutions are far from blameless, but their weakness can be corrected, whereas the mistake in a central department results in social injustice to thousands, and is difficult to remedy. The modern world is distinguished by specialization and differentiation, and this is what makes the organization of our social services so necessary, and this is also why intelligence and understanding must be brought to the devising of new policies and new ways of dealing with questions as they arise. A community which has lost its sense of freedom and security is no real community, and if we are to maintain our sense of social solidarity the State will have to learn to deal, not with isolated problems, but with the life of the citizen as a whole. "Every society," said Mr. Asquith on one occasion, "is judged and survives according to the material and moral minima which it prescribes for its members."

The Unemployment Assistance Board has now added to its functions the care of all who are outside insurance. The local Public Assistance Committees will then no longer be responsible for the so-called able-bodied poor. This is a large class of unfortunate people of all ages up to sixty-five, some of whom are too sick or infirm to work, although not in institutions. Some have never worked at all and some are never likely to work again. A few at least of the youths in the schools from sixteen to eighteen years of age have never had much chance of getting work, although we hope that their chance is increasing every day, but they are not trained and some of them do not seem to wish to be trained. It does seem a little strange to hand them over to an authority which is presumably to deal with unemployment and no one yet knows whether these new responsibilities can be wisely discharged by the Unemployment Assistance Board. Some of these people no doubt are to blame for the position in which they find themselves, but many of them ought to be given humane and sympathetic consideration if our idea of security for every citizen is to be more than a shallow pretence. There are cases of poverty due not to unemployment but to other causes, and these include mothers and children and elderly people who cannot be expected to play their part in gainful occupations. It is difficult to see what can grow out of such confusion, but we may be allowed to say that unless the administrators of the Act have a clearer view of the future than at present it seems probable that further legislation will be required. In any case it is only the local committees who will be in a position to understand and deal with all the individual applications for assistance.

The poverty against which we war is linked up with malnutrition, ill-health, bad housing, and crime, as well as bad management. On the economic side it must be regarded as a fruitful cause of inefficiency and waste. The greater the poverty of the worker, the less purchasing power there is. An increase of purchasing power has its effect upon the trade of the whole nation. Poverty is no longer regarded as an act of God, although I did once, many years ago, hear a worthy Dean of the Established Church say that "poverty was one of God's standing orders." Today we are able not only to measure and assess poverty, but also to discover certain of the causes of poverty while we still seem unable to remove those causes. There is a growing feeling on the part of the nation, a feeling perhaps engendered by the comradeship of the war, that people who suffer from great poverty are suffering injustice and that this injustice must be removed.

It is important when we are discussing poverty to remember that there are various forms and degrees of poverty. What is poverty in one country is not in another, and to a lesser degree what is poverty in one part of the country may not be poverty in another part; but by taking into account the amount of food that is required both for adults and for children, by scientifically examining groups of children with a view to discovering their heights and weights, and how far they have reached a requisite standard, by taking also into account what we consider to be the minimum in the matter of clothing, of food and housing, we are able to say just how far sections of the population fall below our minimum. We have estimates by Rowntree and Professor Bowley, the British Medical Association and others, of what should be a minimum standard as regards food. We are now trying to determine by means of the Slum Clearance and the Overcrowding Acts what should be the minimum of accommodation as regards housing.

In order to satisfy the needs of the average working-class family there must be proper housing accommodation, accessibility for employment, accessibility for services like transport, and especially in the case of children, adequate nutrition. There are still districts where few of these conditions are observed. Almost every house is overcrowded, without proper sanitary accommodation and without baths. All washing has to be done and dried inside the house, and nearly all the houses are in a state of bad repair. Moreover, it is very difficult to get the evils remedied because the tenants are afraid, if they complained, of being turned out. In most of these cases 10s. is what the family would be paying for the inferior accommodation of two rooms without any of the amenities which are suggested as necessary. All this means poverty, and poverty that depresses and destroys any sense of security. The evils we complain of are now being remedied, but it will be some years before we see the disappearance of the slum.

When we are dealing with social security and contrasting what we have done with what has been accomplished by other nations, we can at any rate claim that our social insurance has saved the nation from the worst of the world depression and averted the hardships from which many States have suffered. Moreover, the huge and regular expenditure of the money spent in unemployment benefits, some £700,000 a week, has been a great help to the home market and tided us over a period at a time when export trade had to a large extent collapsed. Social security, therefore, for the average man can be demonstrated to be sound from an economic point of view. It is true that we in England lay great stress on the humanitarian side, but a good defence can be made for this vast expenditure on social and economic grounds.

The remedy suggested by the orthodox economist is to impart more flexibility into the costs structure of our industries, the argument being that by reducing wages sufficiently we should be able to sell our goods overseas and expand our export trade. One economist in a recently published work says: "In the long run there is neither unemployed capital nor unemployed labour." The natural reply is "How long is the run and how great is the cost meanwhile?" Unfortunately there are many other reasons why export trade has decreased and we have only to remember currencies, quotas, and tariff barriers of other nations to see that this argument is not conclusive. The opposite method is to set on foot large-scale relief works and here the problem is to find works that will be in a real sense constructive and reproductive. It is absurd to give work just for the sake of giving work, and it is desirable that any such work should either directly or indirectly increase the wealth of the nation. Still, the revival of agriculture may do something to remove a fair number from the unemployed register, and a shortening of the hours of labour is advocated by the trade unions. We cannot ignore the fact that a very large number, and probably some millions, stand in need of increased purchasing power. Even from the nutritional point of view this is obvious, and from the social and economic point of view there can be little doubt. Whether the proposal is to increase the purchasing power of some millions by wage cutting as suggested by some economists, or by heavier taxation, or by inflation, in all these three cases it must be a hindrance rather than a help and scarcely requires any argument except perhaps in the case of inflation. It is no good trying to create fresh purchasing power by destroying that which already exists. It is often contended that there is a great deal of waste in the distributive mechanism, and it is true, just as to a smaller extent it is true on the productive side. If this waste could be eliminated, and if direct labour costs could be reduced, we might see an increased turn-over, an increase in the earnings of labour as well as a reduction in the price to the consumer. In order to increase the output of labour, which would enable us in the end to employ more people, we have at the same time to increase the quality of employment, and we can only do this by giving the worker shorter hours, holidays with pay, and eventually a share in management, so that all friction will be removed and every inducement given to increase output, lessen sickness, and create goodwill.

Side by side with such methods of enhancing the status of labour, should be the removal from employment of men who have reached, say, sixty-five years of age, and in certain cases sixty. This can hardly be accomplished without a system of pensions, and here the employer must step in and do his part, as in the cases of certain well-known firms throughout the country. There are over 1,000 firms engaged in industry, commerce, transport, banking, etc., which have pension schemes. These schemes vary greatly, some are excellent, and some are not so satisfactory, but they all help to give young or old more security and thus fulfil a useful purpose. The latest of these schemes is that of the Imperial Chemicals Industry. In this case 43,000 employees have been offered the chance of contributing and 80 per cent have already joined. Retirement by right on a pension is at sixty-five and by consent at sixty. I ought to add that hundreds of employers give some share at least of the profits of their industry in various forms of co-partnership, and a recent example is that of Lord Nuffield, who has handed over shares worth £2,125,000 to his employees. All this creates goodwill and certainly gives a sense of security in industry.

The problem of old age is a difficult one, because it is not merely a problem of old age. It is sometimes a question of employment, sometimes of maintenance, but the present generation must face this question all the more so because the number of old people is increasing. Modern methods of industry seem to imply that more men are discharged owing to age than was formerly the case. Fifty years ago the total number of men and women who were sixty-five or over in England and Wales was 1,200,000. Now the population of the aged is nearly 3,000,000 and all the while the number is increasing while the number of young people is decreasing. The problem of the aged is therefore gaining in importance. We find, if we examine the unemployed figures intensively, that a very large number of men are on the margin of the labour force, that is to say, they are over sixty and either approaching sixty-five or over sixty-five. It is generally admitted now that a very considerable portion of the men of sixty-five years and over, whether they are entitled to a pension or not, are unable to compete with the younger men in the labour market. The system of pensions in this country is of two types. The first is the non-contributory State pension of 10s. a week available for aged people of seventy years, but subject to a declaration of means. A married couple, for example, may claim the pension without reduction at seventy years of age if their unearned income does not exceed 30s. per week; if, on the other hand, they are able to earn money and their earnings do not exceed £1 a week above the 30s. allowance, they are still entitled to claim. If their earnings exceed £1 a week, but do not exceed £2 a week, they are entitled to a reduced pension. This is the Old Age Pension Act of 1908. In talking to Mr. Asquith on the subject of old age pensions in 1907, the writer pointed out that there were hundreds of thousands, including agricultural labourers, who could not save for old age and who must be a heavy drain on the resources of their equally poor children. These free pensions have grown considerably. There are now more than 800,000 people in the United Kingdom drawing these pensions at a cost to the Treasury of over £22,000,000. This is more than double the amount that was anticipated at the time. We have in addition to the non-contributory pensions the Act of 1925, The Widows, Orphans and Old Age Contributory Pensions. These are payable between the ages of sixty-five and seventy, and the present number of persons in receipt of these pensions is 700,000, the annual cost being about £18,000,000. The number will no doubt rise in ten years' time to 800,000, involving a cost to the nation of £23,000,000. Old-age pensioners under the contributory scheme, when they reach the age of seventy, draw their pension entirely at the expense of the State, and in their case there is no test of income, residence, or nationality. Over

765,000 persons are included in this arrangement at a cost to the Treasury of some £19,000,000.

The social services which help to give security to the citizen include, of course, education and public health, unemployment exchanges, training centres, schools and hospitals, doctors and nurses, but it is the social insurance services, subsidized by the State and by employers, which have helped so much to relieve the mind of the worker from great anxiety in time of sickness and unemployment. Those who receive the benefits from these services receive them as we have stated before, as a contractual right in respect of contributions paid and for the most part those who receive these benefits may be said to need them. The great majority of the wage-earners of this country are safeguarded in this way, but in addition to these social services there are also social assistance services which give aid according to need. These services include public assistance in all its forms, allowances from the Unemployment Assistance Board, non-contributory old age pensions, free meals for necessitous school children and maintenance allowances to school children. We may add subsidized housing, as is the case with the Slum Clearance Act, or grants in aid and the milk in schools scheme, which also give in an indirect form assistance, all make for security. We shall soon see free milk, or milk at cost price, for all elementary school children. Most of us can remember the time when none of this help was rendered to the average citizen, and since 1890, less than fifty years ago, the cost of public social services has multiplied nineteen times and the cost to the State fourteen times. Leaving out war pensions entirely, the cost per head to the State has multiplied ten times. A large part of the cost of social services, borne by employers and employed, reduces the cost to the Government in that special department, so that only about one-tenth of the national government expenditure on the social services would go to social insurance. Looking at these services from the point of view of the people who benefit, we may say that social insurance covers a large proportion of the wage-earners and their dependents, that is to say, between 26 and 36 millions. Those who receive social assistance would amount to some 1,500,000, also including dependents, but these would not all be the same people and perhaps 3,000,000 may be regarded as receiving assistance in the course of the year. There are also about 5,000,000 people living in subsidized dwellings and about 3,000,000 children getting milk in schools either free or at cost price, with the aid of a grant by the Milk Marketing Board. In addition over 400,000 school children receive free meals.

It will be seen, therefore, that however many the social services, nearly all of them bear upon this problem of giving security, and although there may seem to be a lack of co-ordination and a conflict of administration, yet on the whole there is not very much waste of time and very little waste of money. However, this complexity of administration must mean that there are some anomalies. An unemployed man gets 17s. a week under Unemployed Insurance together with an allowance for his family, while if he is sick he gets 15s. a week under Health Insurance and no help for his family—although, as a matter of fact, his family may need help more when he is sick than when he is unemployed. There was a hiatus between the School Medical Service and the age of entry into Health Insurance, but that gap was bridged over in 1937. There is also the question of what can be done for the dependents of sick insured people who are omitted from the Health Insurance Scheme.

We are now making an attempt to deal with poverty due to chronic unemployment. This will be found chiefly in the special areas. It is a problem not so much of the Midlands or of the South as of sections of the North and Wales. It was especially to satisfy conditions in these areas that public assistance relief was modified, and it was a mistake, perhaps, to set up national machinery for this purpose. Various methods must be devised to suit various needs. We can hardly apply exactly the same machinery to districts that have over 40 per cent of unemployed as we can to towns in the South, where the unemployed may range from 7 to 10 per cent. The truth is, of course, that when the problem of the special areas moved the Government to action, they had no very definite plan, although they were prepared to supply financial aid. It was an experiment which they felt should be made. In so far as they made it the business of a Commissioner to deal with these special areas they were right, but it is questionable whether his functions should have been so limited, whether even now it might not be well to enlarge his powers, to enable him to set on foot more constructive schemes of relief. What is wanted is not so much increased financial support for the relief of poverty as an attempt to provide constructive schemes which will make unnecessary the provision of what may be called salvage services. What we have done in this direction is all to the good.

The Special Commissioner for England and Wales has spent or earmarked nearly £4,000,000 for direct and indirect relief, and £3,000,000 is still available. The indirect relief has been administered by such organizations as the National Council of Social Service. The direct relief consists of grants for drainage schemes, new roads, new bridges, harbour and estuary improvements, trading estates in the North Eastern area, and at Pontypridd and Port Talbot in South Wales, the removal of a part of Woolwich Arsenal to Bridgend in South Wales, and a new aircraft factory in the same area. The Land Settlement Association has also received a large amount of assistance, enabling them to buy estates in various parts of the country and to transfer the unemployed and their families from the special areas and settle them in small-holdings on these estates. Some 2,000 holdings have already been established. In addition to the above expenditure, steps in regard to outside areas which may affect special areas are a loan of £35,000,000 to the London Transport Board, and £26,000,000 to be used by the main line railways for improvement. The benefits arising out of these loans, so far as the unemployed are concerned, are contained in clauses of the contracts which are conditional on work being given to special areas wherever possible. Recently orders have been given to the North-Eastern shipyards for ships for the Royal Navy, and the North will also benefit by munitions for the national defences, costing nearly £70,000,000. Meanwhile the number of insured workers employed has increased by 1,500,000 since June 1932, and in the North-Eastern divisions wages have increased by £500,000 a week. Why should not the Government help to establish by the loan of money at a low rate of interest a couple of hydrogenation plants in South Wales? It would give additional work to thousands of miners, apart from the 2,000 men engaged on each plant. Transference of labour to other districts and towns is inferior as a method to the creation of new industries in these districts.

We have lately witnessed a considerable revival in shipping. If only the fear of war could be removed and trade barriers broken down, we should have something like a boom in world trade. The ports of England would naturally benefit and the deepening of the channels and up-to-date equipment for these ports is long overdue. We are singularly fortunate in this country in having so many ports well situated and of great value to our export trade. Employment could be given to very large numbers of men in effecting the improvements that must be made if we are to cope with a largely expanded trade with other countries. The very fact that these improvements have been effected would help in that expansion.

There are many other ways in which we could give more security to our people: security of work, security of life, and security in old age. We could, no doubt, if we were willing, put an end to poverty, except perhaps such poverty as is due to moral causes, although even so it is difficult to say where the fault of the community ends and the fault of the citizen begins. In principle we all agree with Stopford Brooke's definition of poverty as "That condition of things in which for lack of means no true development of life can be attained." Would that the statesmen of the Great Powers might at long last turn aside from their preoccupations with schemes of war and increased armaments and consider the important problems arising out of poverty, the economic barriers to a full and a secure human life. The resources of civilization are not exhausted. Emerson was right when he said, "We think our civilization near its meridian, but we are yet only at the cock-crowing and the morning star."

CHAPTER V

THE FUTURE OF INDUSTRY

We move in a world of rapid change and conflict. The whole structure of Society creaks under the weight of old and worn out ideas, ready to fall. Must we lie among its shattered ruins, or have we something to replace it? We are swept like frail barques on the crest of a mighty tide. Can we control its dynamic forces? Can we build order out of chaos, hope out of despair, realization out of futility?

T. W. HILL, M.D., D.P.H.

THE complete security we desire for every citizen cannot be obtained apart from social and industrial reconstruction. It would seem, therefore, that changes, however gradual in character, must take place, and some are even now shaping themselves before our eyes. The State is feeling the impact of new ideas and recognizing the new spirit in industry. The pessimists are saying that our social system is outworn and obsolescent. They foresee the upheaval of primitive forces just awaking to life. They tell us that a wave of Communism is sweeping over Europe and that we shall not escape. Dictatorship or Communism are the alternatives they offer to us. Few people accept the view that we are heading straight for Communism and disaster, or believe that the British nation will ever consent to a dictatorship. We are too sober-minded to desire any violent revolution. The average citizen is interested in the Cassandras who prophesy evil, but his inclination is to forget them with alacrity. The Briton is a curious creature, an enigma to the foreigner. He is always predicting a catastrophe, but he never believes in it. Undoubtedly great changes are taking place, but for the most part they are taking place quietly and peacefully, and one such change is the relationship that exists between politics and economics. It has been said that economic needs should determine public policy. At present we are agreed that our social and political system does not satisfy our economic needs and unless we are content with the ultra-individualistic view, it is obvious that public policy must be changed and adapted to meet present-day requirements. Many articles have been written on the subject of poverty in the midst of plenty, and we still have to discover why the expansion of production should not be possible to enable those fundamental wants that are unsatisfied to be enriched by this increase in wealth. If all the resources of the community were available and controlled in some way by public authority, should we see an end of poverty and hardship which today vex the mind of every thoughtful person? The State is intervening in many directions, not so much to check the economic activity of the community as to relieve the suffering and disintegration which results from the unsatisfactory working of the system. There are many who still believe that to interfere in any way with the competitive system is a mistake, and they have the support of certain well-known economists; but, on the other hand, competition which is governed and guided solely by the idea of profits is far from being a complete success.

In speaking of unemployment I have often pointed out that we can hardly expect the unco-ordinated and unregulated decisions of a multitude of producers to provide us with equilibrium in the matter of output, and the problem of distribution seems to be altogether beyond our comprehension. If prevention is better than cure and it is something more than a phrase, then no Government can stand by and merely relieve the hardships arising from individualistic enterprise, instead of attempting by clear, positive leadership to give direction to our economic life. The State has begun to accept various extensions of these responsibilities and is exercising control in many directions, but often control comes too late or is too one-sided. This gives rise to friction and discontent at the slowness of reform.

The ideals of politics and economics should now be recognized as in the same category. We have in this country a large amount of political and religious liberty. What is wanted now is a more definite movement towards economic liberty, for multitudes are the victims of narrow and impeding circumstances, over which they have little or no control. Aristotle said that States are brought to ruin and anarchy by inequality. There is not much fear of anarchy, we are too deeply rooted for that, but there is much inequality and some of it is quite unjustifiable by any known standard. We aim at equality of economic opportunity, for we all recognize that totalitarian equality, as human beings are constituted, is impossible. The distribution of wealth in a well-ordered State should aim at realizing economic justice. The fact that this desire for "equality of opportunity" is growing need not distress us. All progress carries its own disquietude. We ought rather to be encouraged than discouraged at the changes which are taking place.

Changes are always taking place. When people talk about living in an age of transition, they seem to imply that there ever was a time when things were peculiarly stable. Great Britain is as stable, perhaps more stable, than most countries, but we remember the Reform Movement of 1832, the outbreak of 1848, and, to go further back still, the Peasants' Revolt of the fourteenth century, the economic disturbances of the sixteenth century, and since then the aftermath of the Industrial Revolution. We are always living in an age of transition although there may be times that are exceptional and full of perils, such as have been witnessed on the Continent during recent years. Democracy is not simply a form of government: it is a stage in human evolution.

Change is imperative in any democracy, and if with Hitler and Mussolini you regard democracy as a kind of disease, what can you substitute for it but autocracy and dictatorship, carrying with them their own nemesis? Fortunately, in this country there is usually some attempt on the part of those who govern us to see the other side. We dislike cranks, but the worst kind of crank is the man who sees one thing so vividly that he is blind to all the other things which alone can explain the one that he does see. We have had for several centuries a distinctive tradition of what I may call toleration. There is a definite trend in the direction of experiments, whether they be legislative, industrial, or scientific. The Englishman is not dogmatic; he is rather inclined to be anti-dogmatic. Without being quite sure of what democracy means, he stresses the value of freedom of speech and action, of individuality. He does not believe in class struggles, nor does he believe that the economic truth rests with any one group in the community. He watches and judges by every-day experience. While he sees the gradual transfer of political power from one section of the community to another, or perhaps we ought to say the gradual diffusion of political power, he is confirmed in his view that what is wanted is an anti-class party. Above all he is a firm believer in evolution, in progress without cataclysm. The antitoxin of revolution is evolution. He sees no hope in insurrectionism; no hope in vast sudden changes, certainly not unless these sudden changes carry with them the goodwill of all classes and are dictated by urgent political and social needs. He believes in the possibility of improvement. He is never quite satisfied, and perhaps, in view of the large accumulations of wealth and the amazing growth of scientific production, he ought not to be satisfied. Higher wages, better education, more real freedom, and more leisure are accompanied by new ambitions and a keener sensitiveness to everything that hinders progress.

A higher standard of life once gained is a reason for new effort and we cannot therefore be surprised by the alarm and hostility which the working classes express when anything seems to threaten the standard which they have already attained. We create new wants and we are apt to grumble that these new wants once recognized become imperious. This higher standard of comfort, of food and clothing, of housing and leisure, should tend to increase and not diminish. It is the fear of losing this standard which provokes revolt. There is nothing like a sense of insecurity for producing unrest, and it is a justifiable source of discontent. This discontent is not, of course, confined to the industrial field; it is not merely a question of friction between capital and labour; the same restless antagonism, the same dissonance of opinion manifest themselves in all branches of our political, social, and religious life. We can hardly, therefore, expect that industry will be exempt. If religious and political inequalities are felt to be socially mischievous, why should not economic inequality be questioned? Increasingly we are being driven to the conclusion that far greater economic equality will have to come in the future and this is now a principle accepted not only by politicians but also by many of our leading industrialists. The growing restlessness of our age, especially in time of business depression, assumes a more consciously political character, so that the test of statesmanship will be the foreseeing and the forestalling of these times of depression and the taking of active steps to prevent the lowering of the standard of life.

It used to be thought that the growth of mechanical science and invention was largely responsible for the unrest of the working classes, and, of course, it is true that at certain periods there has been a feeling abroad that the machine is governing the man and the man is not controlling the machine. In periods of great unemployment this feeling is most in evidence. My belief, however, is that today it is not so much fear of the machine as fear of the machine when it is held solely by private interests and in private hands. Ownership of the machine combined with ownership of the land might quite conceivably be employed to the destruction of a free democratic society. Just as the machine created the labour organization, so it may be used to disintegrate and overthrow that organization unless it can be shown to be working in the interests of all sections of the community.

While I was in New Zealand, many years ago, a member of the New Zealand Government made this statement: "We mean to organize all our great industries so that they shall not be used to make individuals rich, but every advantage of cheaper services or cheaper products shall go at once to the whole body of the people." This sounds so like an ideal social system that I am reminded of a saying of a distinguished mathematician: "This branch of mathematics," he said, "has never been disfigured by any practical application." We may be, and probably are, heading for Socialism and it needs a little intellectual sympathy to understand it, but the opportunity is offered to us as it is not offered to many peoples to prove that we can co-operate with one another, that labour organizations and business management need not be divorced, and that a common working basis of industrial reconstruction is still possible. We cannot acquiesce in the *status quo* when we are considering the great national services like railways, or mines, or the smaller industrial enterprises less in need of public control. Not only is constant watchfulness on the part of the State required, but also a frank recognition that in every department of our business and industrial life there are common interests. The spirit of partnership must be recognized and even if it demands a profound social reconstruction, measures of practical co-operation will be discovered if only we have the courage to take the next step and willingness to judge the many questions which will arise from a national point of view rather than that of immediate private interest.

When we talk of industrial organization we generally have in mind organization from the point of view of the employer, and we take it for granted that on the side of labour there is already organization; but a completed organization would mean that employers and employed are working in harmony, planning for the future and understanding the difficulties that confront both sides. Every observer of industrial disturbances and social unrest must have come to the conclusion that purely chaotic forces in the industrial field are sure to lead to disaster. We cannot trust to competition either to give us satisfactory economic results or to remove the causes of disorder which are apt to manifest themselves. Unrestrained competition, so far from removing the mischief, is likely to intensify it. The organization of the future, therefore, must be planned to include labour, and the sympathetic co-operation of labour is absolutely necessary if we are to have industrial peace.

But how is this sympathetic co-operation to be obtained? Not by force or sheer compulsion, which sooner or later will break down in industrial enterprises, just as it will break down in the international sphere. It is only by a slow process of education that the best results can be achieved, and by education we mean not only the education of the worker but also the education of the employer. The two must meet one another in a regular and systematic way. The trade union leaders must be taken into the confidence of the employers. They should be instructed as to the exact position of each industry. The difficulty of market conditions, of currencies, of costs, should be explained. Where the profits are high there should be no attempt to conceal the fact, but arrangements should be made by which the employees in one form or another receive their share of the benefits of improved trade and these higher profits. The latest illustration of this co-partnership is the gift by Lord Nuffield to his work-people of shares in the Morris companies to the extent of £2,150,000. We do not deny that those who are at the head of industrial organizations should receive an adequate reward for their foresight and their energy, and fair-minded men will not deny them that reward, but at the same time there must be a genuine application of some system of co-partnership which will be conditioned, of course, by the nature of the business itself. Just as the employers ask to be protected from capricious and unwarranted cutting of prices due to intensified competition, so labour in the same way desires to be protected from unjustified cuts in wages. It must always be remembered that the essential thing in the minds of the employees is a permanent wage, high enough to enable them to live with some degree of comfort and security. This implies that there should be no great fluctuation in prices. The best thing for the economic life of the nation is that the price of goods and services should remain steady. This is quite as much in the interests of labour as of the employer. Powerful industrial concerns may be able, quite possibly, owing to their reserves, not only to pay dividends to their shareholders, but even to incur losses without great hardship; but labour as a rule has very slender reserves and a decrease in wages may mean real suffering to the families concerned. The working man dreads unemployment and low wages, because it means lack of security, not only for himself, but for his wife and children. We have been saved from revolution in this country by our attempt to give some sort of security to labour in bad times by insurance legislation and our social services. Successive Factory Acts have undoubtedly lessened the spirit of industrial unrest. We need to move still further along this road.

If we may take for granted that there is a growing goodwill as between employers and employed, we still have to face the question as to how far the State should intervene in the problem of organized monopoly likely to eliminate competition. The concentration of industry which is a feature of modern times has, of course, an immense bearing on the future. Socialists have been in the past inclined to think that the more concentration in industry the better; that the more monopolies are encouraged, the more likely it is that the State would be able in the first place to control and in the second place to assimilate. This question of monopolies, and the price problem attaching to it, is becoming a serious matter of discussion. Large industrial concerns see the importance of coming to terms with like firms on the Continent, or of establishing there factories and workshops which will give them an international position and enable them to regulate prices. They might conceivably do away with all competitors, and in that case the State would have to step in and act on behalf of the consumers; or again, the State might feel it necessary to intervene on behalf of the weaker competitors who are being squeezed out in the struggle. To some this is merely a side of evolution, to others it is a flagrant violation of economic policy calculated in the end to destroy the peaceful working of industry.

There are two schools of economists taking different views on this subject, the one advocating monopoly as leading to greater State control and the other advocating competition as likely to reduce costs. We must distinguish, however, between combinations implying monopoly and price raising, and that concentration of industry which is known as "rationalization," which means in effect just the application of more economical methods, the taking advantage of improvements in technique, employing more efficient machinery and thereby increasing the power for mass production and distribution. No doubt the war intensified this movement, which was led by the United States and followed by Germany and ourselves. Rationalization, however, does not necessarily mean a better distribution of the social products, although it does mean a larger output, but because it means a larger output it therefore necessitates an increasing demand. The argument runs thus: the bigger the output, the cheaper the product, the cheaper the product, the greater the demand. The trouble is that this does not go on *ad infinitum*, and we must not be surprised, therefore, if in some cases we find what may be called over-rationalization. Nevertheless, there is no likelihood of any return to the old economic conditions, to smaller units, or to decentralization. We have now a policy of concentration which we may use rightly or wrongly. The danger is that it may lead to over-production and therefore to unemployment. To avoid this danger we call planning to our aid.

A definition of political and economic planning has been given as follows: "Positive planning may be defined as the working of a number of organizations in conjunction with one another for some consciously accepted end." There is a sense, of course, in which planning has always existed. Every employer tries to look ahead and to foresee the future, and he will, if he is wise, take steps to that end. An employer said to me the other day: "I bought huge quantities of leather when leather was very cheap and a drug on the market. I am now reaping the benefit when leather has gone up in price and when certain classes of leather are hardly obtainable"; but this is foresight and hardly the planning which economists have in mind. Planning so understood means laying down principles of action by which we may secure a juster balance between demand and supply. It may be necessary to control production or distribution. It may even be necessary to control both. In any case planning means the very reverse of that system of economy which believes that the best results can be obtained by the automatic working of competitive forces. The most important function of planning, therefore, would be not only to regulate production according to a definite programme thought out and laid down, but to study market conditions and trade tendencies for some considerable time ahead with a view to modifying or adapting the programme. No doubt this would be an easier task for the big companies or trusts, because they are able in a general way to influence the markets, and they are capable also by reason of their world-wide ramifications of forming a general idea of what is likely to happen both here and abroad. It is probable that big businesses will in the future always have on their boards one man who is trained by his knowledge of economic conditions to forecast the future. Given a huge industrial concern, concentrated in a comparatively few hands, it should be possible to plan results some distance ahead. As examples we may give the manufacture of steel rails, of motors, and building materials.

There is a movement on foot, led by Mr. Harold Macmillan, to obtain legislation for what is called self-government in industry, the idea being to give compulsory powers to a majority of producers in any industry to enforce schemes of reorganization on smaller and weaker concerns. The general object in the minds of the promoters is to obtain greater efficiency and eliminate wasteful competition, and, of course, to facilitate the production and distribution of the product. Those who plead for this change in our national policy would, like most of us, repudiate the hypothesis of general over-production, but they assume, and the assumption is hard to dispute, that under present circumstances the productivity of the world has increased beyond the power of absorption so far as existing markets are concerned, and Mr. Macmillan attributes the fall in prices which took place previous to the publication of his book as due to this cause. It may be, however, that he has not taken sufficiently into account either the part played by money in this fall or the world depression which still prevails. The very fact that there has been recently a tendency to absorb a much larger increase in production rather strengthens this view. Where he is on certain ground for some time to come is in his contention that the nationalistic policies pursued by other countries have influenced the British Government in the direction of a protectionist economy. It follows, therefore, that he would eliminate competition both internal and external. The disequilibrium between production and consumption would then be resolved. International competition in a very limited market is no doubt wasteful, and international competition may tend to destroy the high standard of living which we accept as necessary. Here he clashes with the views of that school of economists which is urging unrestrained competition and a *laissez-faire* policy as the only way out. Therefore, the plan, as stated in his book, is to maintain a stable system of production and consumption by protecting and regulating each industry. This will mean giving powers equivalent to monopoly, but only to those industries which could be efficiently organized on a national basis. There would be, therefore, a sort of federation of industries under the control of national councils possessing statutory powers.

Perhaps here we may be allowed to interpolate that it looks uncommonly like the "Corporate State" in Italy on the industrial side. Each industry would be a self-governing unit and the policies of the different industries co-ordinated by a Central Economic Council or alternatively an Investment and Development Board. This would have parliamentary powers and would be a kind of industrial parliament. It is easy to foresee that the formation of such national industrial councils and the amalgamation of the numerous factories and plants now under separate ownership would be a gigantic task and naturally would meet with great opposition from smaller organizations. Mr. Macmillan does not worry about method. He contends that each industry could decide this for itself. It follows that, if we are to have planned production in this country and complete amalgamation in each important industry, we should be compelled to plan our foreign trade on protectionist lines, otherwise our carefully laid plans of consumption balancing production would be overthrown. This would mean more tariffs, a system of quantitative regulations, and a kind of clearing-house for imports and exports, thus creating a machine for maintaining a stable productive system. It may be that he could protect the home market and to a large extent maintain a balance in our foreign trade, but it is not so clear that he would be able to protect our export industries. He wishes to prevent our goods being sold abroad at low prices, but whether he could enable our producers at home to sell their goods abroad at a price that would repay the industry is open to much doubt. His remedy would be to subsidize producers, and subsidies would therefore become a permanent part of our economic system. In order to gain the consent of the trade unions, he would have them represented on the Central Economic Council, and they would be reorganized and so far as possible amalgamated in industries. He advocates a regular consultation between management and labour, but there is nothing new in this and, indeed, whatever plan we may adopt of industrial reorganization, such consultations are bound to come and to a considerable extent exist even now. This would mean so great a change in the structure of British industry that it would be necessary to obtain the sanction not only of the Government, since it would mean legislation, but also of all the interests concerned, including the consumers who are so often overlooked. Apart from the consumers, all the partners of any fair reputable system of self-government in industry must give consent to such a drastic elimination of competition. There is always a danger of the more powerful firm directly or indirectly obtaining a commanding position, unless the control by the Ministry of Labour is impartial and just. Too much control would probably arouse the criticism of the owners as against the Government. The main interest of the Government, if such an Enabling Act passed, would be to keep the balance fair as between the collective industry and the community as a whole. No industry would be compelled to enter the unified body of owners, but there would be some disadvantage in being left out, especially if the section happened to be weak. It is clear, also, that the consent of at least a fair majority of the owners must be obtained before any such Act could operate. Then, again, the administrative staff and the wage-earner would be entitled to ask that too much power was not given to the governing body of directors, and the trade unions especially would have to be assured that their position was not weakened.

It is argued that, by such a change in the industrial structure, although you cannot, of course, influence world-wide economic development, you can take account of such developments, and in your own country, at all events, you may be able to fix an appropriate standard both of wants and of supplies. Some industrialists would also argue that you can create a mass demand along certain lines, producing goods that are more uniform in nature in order to enable planning for production to be carried out. The inference is that people who will pursue other methods less uniform in nature will have to incur the greater costs and the increased overhead charges. It is an argument which few of us would care to accept reservedly, especially in the case of products that are manufactured for foreign markets. You may be able to dictate to your own people, you can hardly dictate to your millions of customers overseas. That has been one of our failings in the past. Over and over again it has been demonstrated that British manufacturers have failed to produce goods of a nature and of a quality which would meet the changing conditions of foreign markets, and when we have failed other nations have profited by our failure. Could we plan consumption as well as production, there is no doubt as to the value both of rationalization and of planning. If you can cheapen the costs of goods that are necessary to a very large number of people you are thereby releasing a certain amount of money which might be used for the satisfaction of other wants which are perhaps incapable of standardization. One thing seems to be quite certain and that is that should there be anything like industrial domination due to the concentration of whole industries, the State will have to take powers to intervene. You are always doing away with a system of free competition and the State must therefore be prepared to control more strictly and to act as a protector of smaller interests and of the consumers as a whole. Oppressive prices to the consumers would sooner or later mean the overthrow of the combinations themselves. If the State does not wish to take the responsibility which collectivism would impose, it must at least see that the exercise of power by such formidable industrial organizations is not to the detriment of the community as a whole.

Sir Richard Gregory, speaking on the cultural and social values of science, said that "Modern technical achievement and scientific thought both foreshadowed a new economic structure for society in which they should be used to exercise a decisive influence on the major policies of the State." Political economists, he complained, "seemed unable to adjust these new forces to the natural needs of human life, but he prophesied that the immense increase in the productive capacity of mankind was forcing society to consider the human consequences of the unlimited resources now at its disposal and also to consider the proposed vital change in the relation of human labour to the processes and products of the world's work. How ironical was the comment on modern civilization that the social reaction to these gifts of plenty was not an increase in human welfare but distress and unemployment. Such consequences were due to the neglect of the application of scientific methods to the solution of social problems." What criticism can be passed on such a statement? Just this, that neither the economist, nor the scientist, nor a statesman who is a combination of both, can be sure of resolving the disharmonies in industry and restoring equilibrium where there is at present disequilibrium, without the goodwill and knowledge of the community as a whole. Supposing that it were possible for us to lay down a plan for placing the economic life of the nation step by step on a firm and stable foundation, can we be sure that we should get the adherence and the cordial assent of even a bare majority of the people? Would they understand what we were driving at, and if they did understand, would they be willing at some sacrifice to place the conduct of all our industries upon an ethical basis? Neither the scientist, nor the economist, nor the statesman is able to help us until there is the disposition to be helped and until a desire for gain at any cost on the part of all classes is surrendered. If co-operation for the commonwealth could take its place it is not beyond the wit of man to devise ways and means that with goodwill could be made effective in all the operations of industry. As the individual advances in knowledge so the outward conditions of his life will gradually be adjusted to a new philosophy, but since the individual himself is dependent upon heredity and training, upon a knowledge of himself as well as the facts of life, it will obviously take some time before we can see a rapid growth of social feeling and note the decay of anti-social action.

But apart from the ethical questions which underlie the whole problem of individualism versus collectivism, there is the difficulty that every change in our own country is complicated by the attitude of other nations. Many countries have no industrial ethic whatever, and in competition with other countries they are apt to think that their own advantage is someone else's loss, and vice versa. Still, lest we should be too pessimistic in our outlook on industry and upon our relationship to one another in society, it must be admitted that a civic conscience is being developed and the individual sense of responsibility both to the city and to the community as a whole has become more acute during the last twenty-five years. This is noticeably the case in connection with co-partnership. The number of firms who are now giving their employees both a share in profits and in management is increasing It is also a very significant fact that many large industrial undertakings see the importance not only of social welfare but also of contributing to unemployed and pension funds. This is indirectly a limitation of dividends which, no doubt, though a matter for the future, is bound to come.

Every change should be evolutionary in character, growing naturally out of the past, not involving large dislocations in trade and carrying with it the general consent of the people. Most of us fear exploitation more than we do collectivism. The fundamental sin against humanity is to use the helplessness of others for private and personal gain. The lesson of industrial history is that the right distribution of wealth cannot be realized until all wealth production is regarded as a partnership in which the partners are tolerant of reasonable ideas and believe in peaceful methods.

CHAPTER VI

THE FUTURE OF THE COAL INDUSTRY

> *King Coal is quite safe on the throne he has occupied for so long, but if he is to be supreme and securely established in the many years he has yet to reign he must adapt himself to the changes in the world around him, changes which threaten his supremacy, and changes which, in a world which is never at rest, will certainly challenge his position and power to an ever-increasing extent in the next few years. Let the challenge be accepted in that spirit and there need be no fear for the future of the coal industry in this country.*
>
> J. P. DICKIE

THE moment we begin to consider the meaning and effect of industrial reconstruction we are confronted with the problem of our basic industries. The two main and fundamental industries for this country are coal and agriculture. It is true, of course, that all industries are interdependent and cannot be regarded in isolation, but some are basic in character and some subsidiary. The coal-mining industry at one time gave us supremacy in the manufacturing world. The United States, with far more extensive coal-fields, did not take the lead until 1899. Nearly all our industrial life derives from coal directly or indirectly. Hence the need for the scientific reorganization of coal mining and its allied industries. We are just beginning to see that this national asset cannot be left to the mercy of private and contending interests. The mines should be, and in the end must be, run in the interests of the whole community and with the utmost efficiency. We have no means of knowing with any degree of certainty how long our mines will last, and, seeing that coal is a wasting asset, it is vital that it should be employed in the most economical way consonant with the maintenance of all our industrial enterprises. It must be remembered that we are in this respect in competition with many other countries, the United States, Poland, and Germany, to mention no others. Germany possesses immense quantities of brown coals or lignites, and their chemists are capable of utilizing such coal for a great variety of purposes, but it cannot compare with our coals which, whether they are anthracite or bituminous, are of vast importance in our industrial life. Like petroleum the best coal is classified by its carbo-hydrogen ratio and it is oil which is to a large extent displacing coal for many purposes. In fact, one of the great triumphs of modern science illustrated by the Imperial Chemicals Industry is the liquefaction of coal in transforming it, by the addition of hydrogen in certain conditions of temperature and pressure, into oil and petrol.

The peak year of production so far as British coal was concerned was 1913, when 287,400,000 tons were brought to the surface. In 1934, which is the latest date for which we have accurate statistics, the amount raised was only 220,728,000 tons, although this is an increase of about 13,000,000 tons on the previous year. The decline in the number of miners employed is due partly to the diminished demand for coal and partly it is the result of more efficient mechanical appliances for winning coal. This decline in the number of miners employed is perhaps the most distressing result of the diminished demand, and we cannot ignore the fact that apart from the suffering involved to the miners and their families, it means a charge of something like £15,000,000 on the Unemployed Insurance Fund. It seems probable that something like 200,000 miners, though all of them are not permanently unemployed, will on the average be idle unless conditions with regard to the export trade completely change.

In considering the future of the coal industry we have to remember that we have practically nothing to take its place in this country, that our water power is almost negligible and it seems unlikely that petroleum will be discovered in any large quantity. Accordingly, it is essential that we should use our coal reserves economically even at the expense of the miner. We are not at all sure how long the oil supplies of the world will last, but we know that many large fields have petered out, whilst the world consumes 200,000,000 tons a year. Clearly the supply is not inexhaustible, and it may quite well be as Sir John Cadman says, that in twenty years' time the oil of the world, which is often used wastefully, will be exhausted, in which case coal will become all the more valuable. Many estimates have been given as to the length of time during which we may expect to be able to use our own coal, but it seems extremely probable that in less than 500 years' time we shall have to import coal from abroad.

There are two main reasons why we should make a more scientific and economical use of our coal reserves. In the first place the careless use of coal, and especially the burning of raw coal with unscientific equipment, entails an enormous waste since it fails to give the amount of light and heat and potential energy which we can obtain if rightly used. Moreover, the burning of raw coal inflicts a serious loss upon the community by reason of the smoke and fumes which pollute the atmosphere. In the second place, to use coal unscientifically or wastefully is to handicap ourselves when in competition with other nations like Germany, which is extremely scientific in its use even of inferior coal. Fortunately we are just beginning to understand the importance of research, both on the chemical and engineering side, and the many new developments which are taking place will no doubt give an impetus both to our manufacturing and agricultural industries.

The total consumption of coal in Great Britain, apart from the export trade, is, roughly speaking, about 161,000,000 tons a year. The largest amount would naturally fall under the head of general consumption, which would include coal used for domestic purposes, some 91,000,000 tons. Gas works carbonize 16,500,000 tons, electricity undertakings use 11,000,000 tons, collieries and railways about the same amount, while blast furnaces, which have been increasing in their consumption of coal, would now consume about 10,500,000 tons. The average cost of production is about 13s. per ton and the average receipts about 13s. 6d., although this was in 1934, since when the price has gone up. Coal-cutting machines and conveyors have both increased during the last few years and coal-cleaning plant, a most important development, is largely on the increase.

In speaking of the right use of coal we ought not to forget that metallurgical coke, which used to be produced in a beehive oven at a great loss of rich gases and oils, has now, owing to the introduction of the recovery oven, made it possible to produce a ton of steel with 30 cwt. of coal instead of about 3 tons. In trying to determine the future of coal we have to ask ourselves how far will oil, gas, and electricity displace it as a form of fuel. It is clear that in this country both gas and electricity are almost entirely derived from coal, and the only question is how far the production of gas and electricity will increase. What is still in doubt is the part that imported oil is going to play in the future of our power-driven civilization. Before, therefore, we can deal with the organization of the coal industry and with such questions as that of central selling, distribution, and private ownership, we have to come to some decision in our own minds as to the future of oil in industry. The latest figures seem to show that we are importing in this country something like 2,500,000,000 gallons of crude petroleum, motor spirit, fuel oil, and lubricating oil. Year by year the importation of oil and petrol is increasing. Oil as a fuel is employed on about half the ships recorded in Lloyd's Register. Last year only 20 per cent of the tonnage constructed was coal-fired. In addition, the rapid increase in the number of motor cars must mean a constant increase in the consumption of petrol. The Air Force demands huge quantities of petrol. In many other directions there is a demand for oil and petrol, and it therefore becomes increasingly important to determine whether the importation of these huge quantities of oil at the expense of coal is necessary. There can be no doubt that oil will be used and, as we have said, increasingly used for a great variety of purposes. Its convenience makes this certain, and whether we are considering the fuel of the *Queen Mary* or of the tens of thousands of motor cars, we can be sure that while oil and petrol are available they will be demanded. The problem that faces us in this country is whether we are to be dependent on foreign imports of oil or whether we can, by utilizing our own coal, insure ourselves against the risk of losing our oil supplies in time of war and at the same time benefit our basic industry of mining. The whole British empire contributes only about 2 per cent of the world's petroleum, although, of course, British money is invested in oil wells in most countries that produce it. It seems very certain, however, that we have very little oil in this country and very little natural gas, of which the United States has such large quantities.

It must not be supposed that oil is in every case displacing coal, even the use of oil and petrol for the internal combustion engine means an additional demand for coal in the construction of the steel work of the engines. The cheapest form of power so far as ships are concerned is the Diesel engine. One ton of oil fuel in this case will go as far as three tons of coal and two tons of oil used for raising steam. On the other hand, the modern liner, which gives such high speed, must use oil fuel for raising steam, and a great advantage is that it is as easy to maintain a high speed with oil fuel as it is to maintain a moderate speed, and no more men are required. It only takes about half the time to refuel the ship as it does in the case of coal, and the operation is cleaner and therefore has great attractions. For the tramp steamer, however, coal fuel is very economical and still has a future. Whether it is true to say that we have now entered upon the Oil Age is a matter on which we cannot speak with absolute confidence, but it is quite certain that the trend is all in the direction of using more and more oil and petrol. We are therefore faced with the probable decrease in the demand for coal and consequently a lessened output, unless we can find some fresh method of utilizing the coal which we possess.

Let us review, therefore, the purposes for which coal is at present being employed and the experiments which are being made in various directions to make coal serve other purposes. Science is coming to our aid in this respect. The researches into the chemistry of coal have led to discoveries which will be of immense value to the industry of this country. The Fuel Research Board, which was set up in 1917 as one of the Research Boards of the Department of Scientific and Industrial Research, has been investigating the nature, preparation, and utilization of fuel of all kinds, and its researches, therefore, afford a valuable guide as to the most economical methods of using not only coal but the other fuels that are at our disposal. Perhaps it would be as well to include in these newer methods the use of pulverized coal which, when mixed with oil, has a good many of the advantages of oil and has been used with great success as a fuel. It is cheap, or relatively cheap. It can compete with oil for price and for certain processes is even cheaper than raw coal. The consumption of pulverized coal has risen year by year and is probably now about 4,000,000 tons a year. The United States uses ten times this amount, but in America pulverized fuel is usually supplied from a central depot, a great advantage to industrial consumers who are reluctant to instal a costly pulverizing apparatus of their own unless they are very big industrial consumers like the Cement and Metallurgical Industries. Whatever may be the advantages of a pulverized coal and oil mixture it seems fairly evident that if we could carry the chemical process a step further and liquefy coal, we have a market ready to hand for all that we can produce provided that it can be supplied at a cost not exceeding that of imported oil, which has to pay a tax of 8d. per gallon. The science of chemistry has now taught us how to manufacture hydrocarbon oils from coal, and experiments that have been made on a large scale seem to indicate that a motor spirit made from our own coal is destined to take the place of a considerable part of the imported article. We already obtain large quantities of benzole or benzole mixture as a result of high temperature carbonization used for the manufacture of coke and gas. The large gas undertakings enable us to obtain benzole both from the gas and from the tar, for it is present in the gas in a vapourized form and can be obtained from coal tar by purification, collecting the vapours that are given off when the tar is heated over certain ranges of temperature. Refined benzole is in some respects superior to petrol, and although only a comparatively few of the gas undertakings recover the benzole, the number is extending year by year, and about 30,000,000 gallons of refined benzole are now sold annually. If all the gas undertakings could produce benzole, this amount would be more than doubled.

Low temperature carbonization also, which is still in an experimental stage, is capable of giving us motor spirit of fine quality and in fairly large quantities, but since the main product of low temperature carbonization is coke or coalite and not motor spirit, it is necessary to apply some method of utilizing the gas and dealing with the tar oils. That method is available in connection with a first-rate gas undertaking but in order to make low temperature carbonization a success not only must there be a ready sale for the coalite but some such method as hydrogenation must be used for the purification of the tar oils that are available in such large quantities. It ought also to be remembered that, unless the coke supplied by low temperature carbonization can be sold as a fuel to take the place of coal, its real value is lost, for low temperature coke is not suitable for metallurgical purposes and has more of the qualifications of a domestic fuel. There seems, however, a ready sale for it at present at a fairly high price. A plant recently opened at Erith by the National Coke and Oil Company can use 150 tons of coal per day and yields 15 cwt. of smokeless fuel per ton, 20 gallons of diesel oil, and nearly 15 gallons of petrol. There is a similar plant in operation at Tipton near Birmingham. The Erith plant cost £80,000 to build and to equip. The two plants combined will provide work for 300 miners.

The method of producing oil and petrol from coal, which is known as hydrogenation, is due in the first instance to Dr. Bergius, who began his experiments by producing coal in a laboratory and not reducing it to a liquid; but it was these experiments which showed him that he could produce from coal liquids similar to petroleum oil. When he added hydrogen under pressure to natural coals he obtained a liquid product hardly to be distinguished from natural petroleum oil, and he took out his patents in 1913. It was not, however, until 1921 that he constructed at Rheinau the plant which has enabled important hydrogenation schemes to be carried out. The coal is pulverized very finely and is then mixed with a heavy oil and a small amount of ferric oxide is added to it. When the mixing is done inside a steam converter it becomes a hot fluid. The ferric oxide helps to bring about the chemical changes and pure hydrogen compressed to about 200 atmospheres is forced into the converter. A reaction takes place between the hydrogen and the coal and the effect is that oxygen, nitrogen, and sulphur are driven out or removed in other forms. There is a certain amount of the ash and the coal left as a residue. For the remainder the hydrocarbon matter in the coal combines with the hydrogen to form hydrocarbon oils. This is a very unscientific way of describing many involved chemical changes. There is left behind in the converter nothing but heavy oil, sludge, coal ash, and a little organic matter, while from the converter itself is drawn off hydrocarbon gases, various qualities of oil, and ammoniacal liquor. The next process is to distil the oils that have been drawn off and refine them until they become motor spirit. There is always a middle oil left, which can either be further refined or used as diesel oil. The hydrogen and hydrocarbon gases are again separated and used once more in the process. In fact, the only thing of importance left that cannot be used again in the process is ammoniacal liquor, which as a by-product is converted into fertilizers. What solid residue there is left is used as a boiler fuel. The sludge oils are mixed once more with more pulverized coal and the hydrocarbon gases give more hydrogen.

I have mentioned that Germany has led the way in many chemical experiments, and it is only recently that on any large scale hydrogenation has been carried out in this country, but the plant installed at Billingham-on-Tees by the Imperial Chemical Industries is regarded as completely successful, although no doubt lessons have been learned which will enable improvements to be effected in future hydrogenation plants. In answer to a question in the House of Commons in August of last year the Secretary for Mines stated that the Imperial

Chemicals Industry had already manufactured 7,500,000 gallons of petrol and had made purchases of tar oils and creosote oil chiefly from the gas industry for hydrogenation purposes. The programme of the Imperial Chemical Industries was to produce per annum 100,000 tons of petrol direct from coal and 50,000 tons from tar products, equal in all to 45,000,000 gallons a year. When the plant was in full operation it was expected that 500,000 tons of coal would be required per annum, representing the employment of over 2,000 miners. In addition large quantities of creosote and low temperature tar would be required.

It is perhaps not sufficiently recognized that the Imperial Chemical Industries is very much helped by being able to obtain large quantities of creosote and tar oils from the gas undertakings. If we may take it for granted that it is possible for the Imperial Chemical Industries to produce at least 150,000 tons of petrol per annum, even a preference of 4d. per gallon would probably insure the sale of every gallon produced. The guarantee under the British Hydrocarbon Oils Production Act of 1934 gives a margin of preference on home produced spirit, i.e. the difference between the prevailing rate of import duty and the prevailing excise (if any) on home-produced spirit. This margin was guaranteed at a minimum figure of 4d. a gallon for a period of nine years dating from April 1935, with a provision that whenever the margin exceeded this minimum of 4d. the guarantee period would be reduced *pro rata*. The current import duty at that time was 8d., and since there was no excise duty, this made the margin 8d., which is, of course, greatly to the advantage of the Billingham undertaking. No change has been made since that date, and if this state of affairs continues, the guarantee period will be reduced to four and a half years and will therefore expire in October 1939 unless, of course, some further change is made in the interval.

It has been stated that the capital cost of starting other plants would be prohibitive and there are many difficulties in the way, but if it is desirable that we should produce our own oil in order to enable us to have something to fall back on in time of war, and if at the same time we could reduce the cost of unemployed insurance in the special areas, it might be worth while for the Government to lend money at a low rate of interest and so enable new plants to be established in these areas. Apart altogether from the large capital cost required, something like £5,000,000 per plant, a real difficulty is the shortage of skilled labour. It would probably be quite impossible to find enough skilled labour to construct a new plant without the importation of such labour from other districts. Since, however, a shortage of skilled hands has now become general through the country, the only alternative would be to train such labour and that is obviously a matter of years. The miners are there to produce the coal, but they could not erect the plant themselves. Another reason why the Government is disinclined to embark upon such an enterprise is the loss of the tax on imported spirit and oil. At present over £35,000,000 is obtained by this tax at the rate of 8d. per gallon. There does not seem very much likelihood of a reduction in this tax, but any large reduction would, of course, have an effect upon hydrogenation.

If we are to lose the benefit of the large sum produced by taxation on imported motor spirit, it must be shown that home-made motor spirit would be of advantage to the nation. The first experiments that were made in hydrogenation showed that the making of home-made motor spirit was costly, but five years ago it was stated to be 7d. a gallon and the probability is that the present cost, which the Imperial Chemical Industries does not disclose, is less than 7d. Oil itself, when imported from abroad, is subjected to a process of manufacture in order to produce motor spirit, and the "cracking" of the oil, as it is called, is an indispensable part of the industry. This may be regarded as a set-off against the production of petrol by hydrogenation. In any case it will be a long while to come, under the most favourable circumstances, before we can produce, say, 500,000,000 gallons of petrol in this country, which is less than one-quarter of the amount imported.

An important point to remember is that manufacture at home means the employment of more miners in addition to those who are engaged on the plant. Supposing that the number absorbed by the plant directly is 2,000, giving work to 2,500 more miners, in addition to another 1,500 men who would be indirectly employed, it can easily be seen that the Exchequer would be far from losing the whole amount of the tax by reason of the saving on unemployment. It is worth while noting in this connection that Germany is increasing the amount of oil which she produces annually from native coal and she hopes largely to eliminate the necessity for the importation of foreign oil.

There is only one other point that we ought to mention in dealing with this problem of hydrogenation. We have said that it might be worth while for the Government, following the example of the Imperial Chemical Industries, to establish other plants in special areas and either lend the money at a low rate of interest or actually appoint industrial boards working with Government sanction and thus encourage fresh enterprises. If, however, the Government does take action and help in the establishment of new plants, it is certainly a question as to whether such plants ought not to be nationally controlled. Should oil be discovered in large quantities in this country, the State will control and will reap the benefit. There does not seem any reason why, in the nature of things, if large quantities of motor spirit are manufactured in this country the State should not also exercise control. We have had an illustration in the electrical industry of how short-sighted was our policy when we allowed companies to spring up in all directions, using their own voltages and charging whatever price seemed fit to them, eventually being dealt with by a costly national grid, leaving the electrical companies still in a rather chaotic condition.

Up to the present the most efficient and economical method of utilizing coal is that of high temperature carbonization. The gas undertakings in this country, numbering about 1,500 and employing 110,000 men, are of the utmost importance from the point of view of coal conservation and also of employment in the mining industry, for it must be always remembered that the demand for coal by the gas undertakings is a regular and permanent demand. At present anything between 16,500,000 and 18,000,000 tons of coal per annum are converted by high temperature carbonization into gas, coke, fertilizers, tar oils, and derivative chemicals. There is very little waste in a first-rate plant, and it is estimated that something like 80 per cent of the heat energy of the coal is utilized by this method. Over 11,000,000 tons of coal are used by the electrical power stations, and here it must be admitted that, valuable as electricity is for a great variety of purposes, it is more costly than gas because so large a quantity of raw coal must be used for its generation. In producing electricity only about 25 per cent of the energy of the coal is obtained and the rest is unavoidably lost.

Both the consumption of gas and electricity tend to increase, and electricity, being a late comer in the field and having the advantage of the national grid supplied by Government money, tends to make rapid progress. This is only natural because it is a late comer in the field compared with gas. On the other hand, new uses for gas are constantly being discovered. There is a very large increase in the industrial field and it is not improbable that it may for heavy vehicles supplant petrol when a sufficient number of gas stations have been established. The more economical the production of gas and the more up to date the plant, the less demand there is, of course, for coal, and here again science, while conferring benefits with one hand, seems to take them away with the other.

The increasing use of both gas and electricity are doing much to purify the atmosphere of smoke pollution. It is estimated that nearly 40,000,000 tons of raw coal are consumed each year for domestic purposes. One cwt. of every ton goes up the chimney unconsumed. If this could be replaced with a smokeless fuel, whether coalite or coke, gas or electricity, it would be a great benefit to the community as a whole. It is estimated that two-thirds of the smoke pollution is due to the domestic hearth, and this, combined with the smoke given off from the industrial chimney, means that in the

London area alone 76,000 tons of soot are deposited every year upon the 117 square miles of this county, and not only soot but sulphur and other chemical products of coal. Apart from the direct loss, we have the indirect loss due to destruction of clothes, of vegetation, and fine buildings, not to speak of the injury to human life, especially in the case of little children. Many of our industrial cities lose half of the ultra-violet rays of the sun. Smoke pollution could be reduced to a negligible quantity and therefore there is all the more reason for the researches pursued by the Fuel Research Board. The production and use of coke-oven gas to which reference has been made has changed the whole face of industry in South Yorkshire, for coke-oven gas is now used by gas-distributing authorities and is accepted as being equal to gas produced by high temperature gas-making plants. The Sheffield Gas Company long ago began to take over and distribute coke-oven gas and at the present time almost the whole of the gas distributed by the Sheffield and Rotherham Gas Companies is coke-oven gas, Sheffield making only 1½ per cent and Rotherham only 3 per cent in their high temperature carbonizing plants. The companies are thus able to offer gas in bulk to large industrial consumers at a very low price, making it therefore unnecessary to use raw coal. It is in this area that there is a notable use of a gas grid. The South Yorkshire Gas Grid Company, representing the coking plant owners and the

Sheffield Gas Company, have laid mains and supplied gas over a wide area to the entire satisfaction of the industrial users.

Turning now to the more national aspect of the coal problem, we are confronted with the anarchy which for so long has reigned in this industry. In order to help the miner there has been a voluntary agreement on the part of large coal consumers to pay more for their supplies; this may have an effect of keeping open the less economic mines. On June 4th Parliament approved the Central Selling Scheme on which seventeen distinct schemes are based. This will do away with some of the extreme forms of competition that have affected the coal industry for many years. The Government has also decided that mining royalties should be nationalized, a long overdue measure which should make possible a much more unified control.

There are three stages in the sale of coal from the pit-head. There is the colliery sales organization, then the wholesaler, and finally the retailer. It may pass through the hands of several retailers and this usually adds to the cost. In any case the method is not efficient. Large buyers are able to get better terms in competition with small merchants, and the largest buyers of all may, therefore, be of little benefit to the colliery. What is wanted is that we should eliminate price cutting and also some intermediate profits, so that the consumer may be satisfied that he is getting his coal at a fair price and one that will not unfavourably affect the miner who produces it. Many coal merchants are not making large profits, but too many are making too large a profit per ton because they are dealing with such small quantities. That is to say, we are trying to support an excessive number of distributors. We ought to concentrate the distributive trade in fewer hands, and if this were done we could reduce the cost of distribution, no doubt, by 3s. or 4s. a ton. The present Act of Parliament regulates production and disposals. It does not sell the coal, it only says where you may sell it and how much may be produced. Each mine has its market quota and one of the difficulties is that the quota for certain qualities of coal may not be large enough to supply certain areas. Whether the Mines Act will prove to be a success depends very largely upon the colliery proprietors. The general principle of the Act seems to be accepted, and what is wanted is that it should be carried out judiciously and in a manner fair to all the parties concerned, since the pooling of receipts renders this essential.

The present concern of the Government is with the problem of the uneconomic mine, of fair prices for the producer, and a fair wage for the miner, combined with the central selling agencies. But we ought not to forget the miner himself, who is killed at the rate of three or four a day, some hundreds being injured during the same period. There are also the diseases caused by mining operations, like nystagmus, a disease which costs the industry hundreds of thousands a year in compensation. The trouble is that the more science comes to the aid of the coal industry and renders it a less arduous occupation by mechanical means, the more likely it is that miners will be put out of work. Coal-cutting machines, driven by compressed air or electricity, lessen the dangers to the miner, but also lessen the need for the miner himself. We may say the same about the mechanical conveyers which have so lightened labour in the pits. There are many other ways in which we can improve the lot of the underground worker, and the Miners' Welfare Fund is a notable illustration, but all the same there does not seem any real remedy for unemployment in the mining industry unless we can devise new ways and means of using coal or increase our exports. Failing that, other employment for the miner himself must be found. In the future it may be that coal will be utilized more extensively at the pit-head both for the manufacture of gas and for the production of electricity. There is no reason in the nature of things why hydrogenation plants should not also be established near the pit-head in coal areas. It is doubtful, however, whether such schemes would enable the uneconomic mines to be worked and, naturally, any attempts to produce either gas, electricity, or oil at the pit-head would be made in connection with coal areas that were economically productive. Most people believe that these uneconomic mines must be closed and that mines should be amalgamated in larger units. Many people also believe that no remedy will be successful apart from the nationalization not only of royalties but also of the mines themselves. That is a question which sooner or later the politicians will have to take in hand. It is improbable that this or any other Government in the near future would consent to nationalize the mines in the sense of actual Government management and control from Whitehall. There does, however, seem every likelihood that in the comparatively near future nationalization in the sense of national control will be realized. In order that a nationalized mining industry should be free from the fluctuations of party politics it might be necessary to set up a Coal Mines Board somewhat on the lines of the London Transport Board. Both the Sankey and the Samuel Commissions recommended ownership by the State and there is growing feeling in favour of this recommendation. Many colliery proprietors would, of course, offer the strongest objection and contend that it means ruin to the industry. On the other hand, there are many owners who see no other way out of this extremely difficult and perplexing problem. The cost of nationalization is also a great hindrance to any rapid action. The mine owners would have to be adequately compensated for they, much more than the royalty owners, have sunk money in the industry and taken risks. The

Samuel Commission put the amount needed for buying the mines, the royalties, the waggons belonging to the collieries and all the works at £350,000,000. It seems rather an exaggerated estimate in the light of present-day facts, and to the outsider the cost seems prohibitive, but no doubt there would be a great saving if the uneconomic pits were closed down and the other pits amalgamated in large units and the whole industry organized with a view to the economic production of gas coke, pulverized fuel, oil and motor spirit, the tar for road-making, the fertilizers, and the wide range of chemicals and dye-stuffs.

Whether you rationalize or nationalize, the industry cannot be left in its present condition, and difficult as is the problem of composing the differences between the large number of competing vested interests, the State will sooner or later have to act and act not only in the interests of the industry, but not less in the interests of the miner himself, who makes the industry possible.

CHAPTER VII

AGRICULTURE

If my book only encourages further dreaming and imagining about the land it will have more than served its purpose, for deep in the inner recesses of man's sub-conscious mind lies the indelible impression of the land—a heritage which, by greatly dreaming and greatly imagining, could be galvanized into a mighty power, capable of strengthening the conscious endeavours of mankind and directing them along paths leading to creative achievement in the spheres of individual happiness, personal health and social justice.

S. G. STAPLEDON
The Land now and To-morrow

AGRICULTURE is for many nations the most basic of all industries and although we cannot, in this country, judge of its importance by the number of people engaged in it, we are aware that any large decline in agriculture must inevitably affect the national health and well-being of the country. We must therefore differentiate agriculture from most industries in that it does require special assistance and consideration, since a high standard of health and physique on the part of the rural population is of vital interest to the State, and we may add that from the point of view of national defence the same thing holds true. Agriculture is something more than a problem of soil culture. It is and has been for some time past the concern of the statesman who finds himself involved in economic questions not easy of solution. For a long period following the industrial revolution agriculture was apt to be ignored and it is only recently that we have come to the conclusion that some portion at least of our national trouble has arisen from the over-emphasis of urban industries at the expense of rural life and the encouragement of agriculture. The neglect of agriculture has been to some extent responsible for unemployment. A hundred years ago, no doubt, it was possible for a man who failed to find work in industry to return to the land, but the more our industries became specialized in the town, the more an agricultural policy was neglected, the greater became the divorce between town and country.

We have to remember that one-third of the total national income is spent on food, and 90 per cent of the land is not urban and industrial in the strict sense. The future of agriculture is bound up with our food policy. A great deal of discussion has been going on on the subject of malnutrition. A sound nutritional policy would lay much stress upon the proper development of our countryside. The standard of living has risen during the last fifty years, but not even yet has nutritional truth filtered down to the poorer classes of the community. There has been a distinct reinforcement of the nation's power to survive periods of stress, and this is of vital importance in face of the dangers to which the modern State is exposed. We have not, however, evolved a clear-cut agricultural policy which would provide all that is required to supply the growing needs of a large industrial population and at the same time strengthen the hold of the agricultural labourer on the soil. We accept the dictum that a prosperous agriculture is essential to a well-balanced national life, but when it becomes a question of maintaining or increasing the rural population, of utilizing and making fertile the waste land, in providing an ample supply of fresh foods necessary to health, we cease to take any further interest in the matter and leave it to the farmer and to the Board of Agriculture.

There are two questions which are a matter of discussion at the present time. The first is whether our policy should be to encourage the production of foods that are especially congenial to our soil and climate, such as milk and live stock, vegetables and fruit, as against cereals and sugar-beet. The second point about which we ought to make up our minds is the part that agriculture ought to play in improving the health and physique of the poorer sections of the population. These two questions are not necessarily distinct, but there is a growing disposition, as a result of the advice of physiologists, to press for a larger production of the right kind of food from the point of view of physique. There is, therefore, an economic question as well as a health question, and if it could be shown that there was a possibility of combining a properly balanced economic life and at the same time encourage the production of food, giving the optimum standard of diet, it would be sufficient to convince our statesmen that more should be done for the development of agriculture.

We may take it for granted that all the evidence goes to prove that this country is particularly suited to produce the greater part of our essential foods. One must qualify that, of course, by saying that so far as cereals are concerned it is quite impossible for us to produce all the wheat we require without using land that is utterly unsuited for wheat production. We could very greatly increase our supply of food, notwithstanding the fact that we still have a large number of farmers who are inefficient cultivators and have neither the energy nor the ability to strike out on new lines and to modernize farming. It is not as though sufficient advice were unavailable; we have at the Board of Agriculture a body of men who are only too anxious to supply information and to give assistance either to the farmer or the smallholder, and we have research stations like Rothamsted, under Sir John Russell, which do more than research work, because they extend to everyone who seeks help the very latest results of their experiments. Sir John Russell himself has no doubt whatever that we could greatly develop food production:—

(1) By increasing the area under cultivation.
(2) By increasing the amount of individual crops and output per acre.
(3) By combining crops into better and more productive systems.

If we could increase our output without increasing the cost of production or raising retail prices, we should greatly advantage the nation by absorbing some, at least, of the unemployed and by supplying the food necessary to build up a healthy population. It ought not to be forgotten that, at the same time, while we are giving employment to men on the land we are also assisting the manufacturer, the makers of agricultural machinery, of fertilizers, and feeding stuffs. Much might be done also to improve the farm buildings which in many cases have been allowed to get into disrepair. Moreover, the production of food means in the end more employment for the bacon factories, the mills, and the tanneries. If all the farmers in this country were prosperous, and if all the farms were as well cultivated as they should be, there are many ways in which additional employment could be given to other occupations than those we have mentioned. In dealing with coal we pointed out how important it is that we should be able to produce our own oil or a considerable proportion of it in the event of war. The same argument would apply to agriculture and the production of food. It may not be possible to store wheat in large quantities in this country owing to the climate, but we can at least have six months' store in hand instead of six weeks. Whether that wheat should be imported or grown here is a matter of doubt, but it is not open to doubt that our output of food could be rapidly increased with proper cultivation.

We are not claiming that the problem of unemployment can be solved by a revival of agriculture, although a few at least of the unemployed could be permanently absorbed. The unemployed agricultural labourers should be our first concern and, with increased production, that at any rate should be possible. If, however, any large number of men are to be absorbed into agriculture they must be trained. It is useless to put people on the land without the necessary knowledge, and credit must be given to the Land Settlement Association, which has taken men from the mining areas and after proper training provided them with smallholdings. These colonies of smallholders are established on a co-operative basis, all the buying and all the marketing being carried out on this principle. Many of the men who have been settled on some, at least, of the twenty-five estates already purchased by the Land Settlement Association have had their own allotments, and with a natural inclination to work on the land they can, with proper training, be made self-supporting. In addition to giving the cultivators an ample supply of fresh and wholesome food, they have a healthy occupation in the fresh air and a certainty for the disposal of their surplus output. It is perhaps too early to say whether all these settlements already established will be a success, but by producing the food for which the land is specially suited and producing it under expert management they are making a most valuable experiment. The Land Settlement is only at the beginning of its work, but already there is hope that a large number of families in which the bread-winner was totally unemployed can be established on the land as producers and enabled to live a better and a more healthy life. When we are discussing smallholdings we ought not to forget the preparatory work which has been done by the Society of Friends in providing allotments and group holdings, the latter being now a department of the Land Settlement Association.

The crucial question, when we are considering a national agricultural policy, is just how far we should reduce the imports of food which, after all, have to pay for our exports, and to what extent this food can be more profitably produced in this country. We must not forget that every reduction of imports affects the shipping interests which bring food in such large quantities from overseas. All the more must we consider this question in all its bearings when we remember that shipping industries in other countries are so often subsidized. The problem is to discover what is to the national interest on the balance. We have invested large sums of money in other countries like the Argentine and in our own Dominions like Canada, Australia, and New Zealand. These investments abroad mean that dividends have to be paid and dividends cannot be paid except by the sale in this country of their agricultural output, which may be and probably is not more than £100,000,000 a year. It is useless to blame our Dominions because they export the very things which they must sell in order to be able to import from us the manufactures they must buy. There are certain foods which we cannot produce in sufficient quantities at home and, moreover, cannot produce them at a price which will enable the British consumer to have the benefit of cheap food. After all, the problem of agriculture is bound up with the welfare of the whole community. It must not be regarded as a case of agriculture first, to the neglect of all other interests, nor must we consider agriculture as being comparatively unimportant—the Cinderella of the industries.

Can an agricultural policy be devised which will take into account all the factors and do justice to all? There are very divergent opinions not only on that question but also as to how the land ought to be utilized to the best advantage. Some people think that large-scale farming is the only way in which farming can be made to pay. Others believe that the owner of a small farm whose interest it is to make the most of it is best able to secure satisfactory results. On the other hand, the small farmer is often unwilling to work with others, and yet it is only by means of co-operation that he can secure the use of the necessary machinery or provide for the proper marketing of his produce. Piecemeal ownership is a mistake, but a large number of comparatively small farms working co-operatively, both for buying and selling, and utilizing machinery and labour to some extent in common, would be able under present circumstances to make farming pay. Large farms will never be successful unless in the same way they can be worked economically. There must be sound management and sufficient capital, and in the case of these large estates it would be better if limited companies were formed so as to escape the heavy death duties which necessarily, in the case of single ownership, mean the depletion of working capital.

There seems little doubt that the idea of co-operation is steadily spreading. Under the Town and Country Planning Act of 1932 it is possible for the owners of farms as well as the owners of land, in conjunction with the local authority, to suggest a plan of development which would mean that several estates were under one skilled management. This implies the right use of machinery and marketing schemes, enabling the owners to get a fair return for their financial outlay. It is also important that costing accounts should be kept. Too often it has been the case in the past that the farmer was unaware whether his farm was paying or losing money, particularly where he was losing money. Today it is becoming customary not only to keep accounts for the purpose of the Inland Revenue but also to analyse these accounts and so discover along what lines it is most profitable to move.

So much interest has been aroused in this question of agricultural prosperity that the time has definitely come for us to consider whether, in the interests of the country, it is not to our advantage to maintain and improve the fertility of the land, to secure an adequate supply of fresh foods necessary to health and nutrition, to provide more work for men who are still unemployed and finally to make sure that we produce all the food that is economically possible as a part of the problem of defence in the case of war. It seems clear that the country is not averse to spending money on agriculture if it can be sure that it is well spent, and that the whole industry is run with at least as much efficiency as any other industry. If we can only afford to spend a limited amount of money on subsidising agriculture, how should that money be spent? This leads one to the problem of arable versus grass land, and here the views of men like Professor Stapledon are of value. He and many of the experts would be in agreement that grass land improvement is necessary for the production of the protective foods, and Professor Stapledon has shown by his experiments that there is an alternative to the subsidizing of crops which he would consider uneconomic. That alternative is the better management of grass land. Lest it should be thought that the good farmer has paid no attention to the improvement of grass land, let it here be stated that for many years he has seen its importance and has done all in his power to bring even poor land up to a good standard, but the average farmer is apt to let things go. He knows very little about new grasses, he has neglected drainage, lime, and fertilizers, and he may not even have heard of grass-drying, which, under proper management, seems to be rather a big issue in the future. It looks as though the time is about due for a revival of the interest in grass lands. As nearly one-third of Great Britain is under permanent grass, it is necessary that this grass should be brought into proper condition, otherwise the grazing is of little value for the live stock. It is useless for farmers to cry out for relief in the shape of subsidies unless they are willing to overhaul their own farming methods. Professor Stapledon, who has given a great deal of study to this question, thinks that the system of permanent grass is a mistake owing to loss of fertility and the risk of disease. His experiments seem to show that, by ploughing up the greater part of this permanent grass, and after a period, resowing it with new grass seed and giving a plentiful supply of lime phosphates and animal manures, such grass lands would become wonderfully fertile. He contends that what has happened is that the soil has been exhausted by continuous cropping, and he is no doubt right; but it is not enough to build up good grass lands, when such expenditure is not justified unless the surplus grass, not consumed by the live stock, can be utilized. Here comes in the whole question of grass-drying, which applies especially to early summer grass. Such grass, if cut and dried, is available for winter cattle food and contains a high protein and carotene content. Cattle fed upon this grass give milk with a full content of Vitamin A. Grass-dryers costing £750 each can hardly be used by the smaller farmer, but they could be used by a group of small farmers and there are possibilities of drying other things besides grass. Such dried grass would enable the farmer to dispense with some, at least, of the purchased foodstuffs for winter feeding.

Provided that it is possible to carry out the recommendations of Professor Stapledon, there is no doubt that grass land agriculture could be made very profitable and that we should be able to produce just the foods in large quantity that Sir John Orr and other scientists think so desirable. Sir John Orr wants to see an increase in the consumption of protective foods to the value of £200,000,000 a year at retail prices, and it is suggested that it might mean giving work to 500,000 people on the land. This, of course, is mere conjecture and in any case progress made in increasing the production and the consumption of food would not be rapid.

Quite recently there has been published a book

called *The Revival of Agriculture.* It is the work of a Committee of the Rural Reconstruction Association and it advocates a National Food Council, representing the interests of the nation as a whole and not merely the interests of the farming community. On such a National Food Council the Government, the producers, and consumers would all be represented and such a body would have to decide how far it was wise to import our food and how far to produce it ourselves. The Council would also have to take responsibility for prices and rates of wages. It would have to decide what cereals should be grown and in what quantity and how far we should try to be independent in respect of milk, bacon, poultry, eggs, fruit, and flowers. The Committee would go so far as to aim at a greatly increased production of wheat with high tariffs on most foods and in certain cases, no doubt, prohibition of import. Agriculture could, of course, be encouraged along these lines, but their claims are exaggerated both as to amount of food that might be produced and to the number of men that would be employed. The figures will not bear close investigation.

It is difficult without fuller enquiry to determine how much we should import from other countries and how far we should grow in this country crops like sugar-beet, which, for its 374,000 acres, receives a subsidy of £2,775,000 and a rebate on excise duties of £2,438,000. The factories are now all united in a single corporation and the subsidy is now limited to 560,000 tons of white sugar per annum. There is a great deal of opposition to this subsidy both in and out of Parliament.

So far as wheat is concerned the Wheat Act of 1932 has laid down the policy, which is to secure a standard price so that a deficiency payment is made to farmers who grow wheat of a certain quality and sell it to the millers. The amount of the subsidy is collected by a levy on the millers and on imported flour. The deficiency payments are so much per hundredweight, and are calculated to give the grower a return of 10s. per cwt., but the subsidy is paid on a limited amount, viz. 27,000,000 cwts.

The other schemes that so vitally affect agriculture were introduced by the Agricultural Marketing Act of 1931, the main object of which was to set up marketing boards to exercise a control over price, production, and processing for specific products. Commissioners have been appointed to deal with pigs and pig products, milk, fat stock, poultry, and eggs. These schemes have to be accepted by the producers and passed by Parliament, and the marketing boards are then elected by the producers. It is an entirely new development in this country and has met with a great deal of criticism, but if control is to be exercised at all, the method adopted must be somewhat along these lines. The difficulty of fixing standard prices is obvious, since the relation between production and marketing brings up the whole question of distribution and the problem of equalizing supply and demand. These questions are being faced and modifications of the schemes will no doubt be introduced from time to time and have, in fact, in some cases been already introduced.

The Rural Reconstruction Committee, as I have said, is in favour of high tariffs or even, in certain cases, of prohibition in order to encourage agriculture in Great Britain. Over against their report we may set *The Agricultural Dilemma*, a report by Lord Astor and Seebohm Rowntree. It is an inquiry, made with the help of agricultural experts, based on the belief that it would be possible by large-scale land settlement schemes, not only to produce much more food, but also to absorb considerable numbers of the unemployed. The result of this inquiry goes to prove that wholesale prohibition of the import of food from other countries or, what is very much the same, high tariffs discouraging such imports, would only create other difficult problems and merely change the nature of our national anxieties. The report does not encourage the view that we could greatly increase the amount of wheat which could be profitably grown in Great Britain. Roughly speaking, we produce 24 per cent of the wheat we consume. If we could produce another 30 per cent, and that would involve a large economic cost, we should still have to depend upon other countries for over 40 per cent, and we should also be using large areas of land for wheat growing which could be more profitably used for other purposes. In fact, wheat growing would tend to decrease in this country were it not for the subsidy by the Board of Agriculture, amounting to £7,000,000 a year. We may say, in fact, that it cost £7,000,000 to increase our home production of wheat from 16 per cent to 24 per cent. The idea that we can be self-sufficient in food supplies is altogether Utopian. It is sometimes argued that this extra wheat production, which seems on the face of it so desirable, would be a help in time of war, but the inquiry tends to prove that it would be far more economical to store wheat for such a possible event than to produce it ourselves. On the other hand, an increased home production of other commodities such as bacon and dairy products would be more profitable, more helpful in time of war, and would not seriously endanger our relations with other countries.

As we stated at the outset, the two questions we have to ask are, firstly, how can we ensure an increase in the consumption of home-produced agricultural products and so carry out what is obviously the wish of the nation in raising the nutritional standard for the poorer class of the community, and secondly, how can we, by increased production of these foods, give employment to a larger number of persons and so help to some extent to solve the unemployment problem? So far as increased consumption is concerned, the increase should be in the direction of more meat, milk, eggs, fruit, and vegetables, which are relatively high-priced commodities and easily produced in this country. The lower the family income, the less of these foods can be consumed, and without raising the standard of wages there seems to be no remedy but a subsidy. The problem here is partly one of distribution. No doubt some economies could be effected in the cost of food distribution, but it is a very complex problem and will require careful consideration and experiment before great changes are made. More economical methods of distribution, combined with a State policy of subsidizing the distribution of protective foods to the poorer classes of the community, might be a partial solution of our social services, and we are now subsidizing agriculture both directly and indirectly. There seems no real reason why, if the physique of the people is so important, some attempt should not be made to subsidize the consumption of such foods as are desirable in the interests of health.

The criticism that has been levelled against the Government that it has dealt with agriculture in a too piecemeal fashion, has in it an element of truth. First one and then another problem has been attacked without taking a broad enough view of the whole industry. Each branch of the industry deplores the omission to deal with its grievances. The farmers may grumble, but they believe that the present Government has made a step in advance by reason of its subsidies and the regulation of production and marketing. It is too late now to go back to unlimited imports, the farmer has either got to be assisted or abandoned, and the probability is that we shall have for some time to come measures of assistance depending upon tariffs and restriction, subsidies and regulation. Already we see the effect, whatever may be the loss to the community, of giving assistance to wheat, potatoes, vegetables, hops, milk, and bacon. The live stock beef and veal will come next and poultry will follow. It is what we may call the methods of experiment, never quite certain of success and yet never incapable of improvement. No doubt there is want of balance throughout the various branches of the industry, but that will remedy itself in time, since the enterprising farmer will look in the direction in which he can obtain the largest remuneration for his outlay of labour and capital. Now that we have embarked upon a system of restriction of imports, it would be as well that the whole matter should be thoroughly explored and that a definite programme should be laid down which could be modified in the light of events. The fear that many of us have is that, if by restriction of imports we rapidly increase home production, in order to help the farmer, we are likely rapidly to increase the price of foodstuffs to the detriment of the consumer. That is what economic isolation means. Our agricultural production has increased by 14 per cent or 15 per cent during the last few years and the cost of living up to the present has not been unduly raised, but the tendency will be for a considerable increase in production wherever any branch of agricultural industry becomes a really paying proposition. We have already seen this in the case of milk and pig production and we now produce nearly all the potatoes and hops that we require.

In other directions agricultural research has made it possible for the farmer, unless he is innately conservative, to take advantage of the new discoveries of science in the direction of manures, improved grass land and last, but not least, feeding stuffs. This means a much higher standard of cultivation and therefore increased production. There is still not enough direct co-operation between the best men in the industry and the Board of Agriculture. It is true that the Board of Agriculture itself is prepared to help, but it cannot help unless the various organized bodies in connection with agriculture are willing to sink their differences and help to define an agricultural policy which will meet the needs of the times and not arouse the opposition of the vast army of consumers. This close co-operation between the Government and the industry is sure to come, and meanwhile the best hope for agriculture is that no irretrievable steps shall be taken which would check new experiments and fresh developments.

CHAPTER VIII

CONCLUSIONS. A BRIEF REVIEW

Reviewing what has been stated in the preceding chapters, we are able to arrive at certain conclusions acceptable *au fond* to the student of economic and social problems. The first is that in matters of the health and nurture of the community the State cannot afford in face of foreign competition to neglect the question of self-defence, and that the first line of self-defence is a healthy and intelligent people. The action of the Government in setting up a Committee for Physical Training and Culture and allocating the sum of £2,000,000 for this purpose, is a proof of the urgency of the problem. Whether we are thinking of the child and the adolescent or the adult, the broad outlines of policy must be the same, a sufficiency of the right kinds of food giving resistance to disease, the physical training which will maintain and increase well-being, the proper housing of the citizen, making possible a true family life. These are indispensable factors in the building up of a strong nation. Employment for reasonable hours at a fair wage for all who are capable of work is therefore essential, since unemployment carries with it the seeds of deterioration. It destroys and saps the morale of the worker and nullifies all the preparatory effort of our health and educational authorities. The ideal, of course, is *mens sana in corpore sano*, but that ideal cannot be achieved without forethought on the part of the State. Theoretically this much has now been conceded. We all recognize the responsibility of the State and the local authority for health, education, and security. It will take time before the theory will be fully carried out in practice, but the nation is in no doubt about the matter and Governments sooner or later carry out the behests of the nation. Already much has been accomplished. The collectivism of today is no longer merely a matter of water and sanitation, with a slight and inadequate protection afforded to the worker. We have reached a stage when we begin to see clearly that whatever our motives there is no such security against foes, whether within or without the State, as a prosperous and contented people.

On the industrial side, the advance has not been so rapid for many reasons, but even here the rigours of competitive life have been considerably modified by governmental and administrative measures. Sometimes these measures have been forced upon a recalcitrant legislature by organized labour, but quite often they have been the result of the Englishman's sense of fair play, not untouched by humanitarian feeling. Even where the fiercest competition prevails we notice signs of goodwill; shorter hours of labour, more leisure and therefore more recreation, better wages and conditions of employment, holidays with pay, profit-sharing and co-partnership, and generally speaking more consideration for the welfare of the employees in industry—these are evidences of a new orientation, a changed point of view on the part of the employers and of public opinion.

No doubt the organized expression of discontent has led to legislation in some of the principal industries, and we have witnessed both in agriculture and in coal-mining some attempt to allay this discontent. For the miner there has been manifested a genuine sympathy on the part of all classes of the community. Sooner or later the steps already taken will have their necessary corollary and this basic industry will be placed fully under the control of the State. Better still, perhaps, would be the recommendation of the Royal Coal Commission to co-ordinate all the fuel resources of the country under a National Board of Fuel and Power. This would include gas, electricity, oil, blast furnaces, and coke ovens. Such a step would make it possible to deal not only with the uneconomic collieries and the inefficient and wasteful use of coal, but also with the problem of the unemployed miners who have been left far too much to the mercy of competitive forces.

The problem of agriculture does not allow of any simple solution. It is true that it is a basic industry, but it is not an industry that lends itself to collectivism. Farmers from time immemorial have regarded themselves as independent units. The farmer is conservative by nature and tradition. He has been accustomed in the past to trust his own skill and judgment. He is dependent, moreover, upon factors which are entirely beyond his control. He must be content to be patient in bad seasons and to work for long periods without seeing fully the fruits of his labour. This encourages the idea of self-sufficiency. Modern agriculture has lessened this self-sufficiency, for the question of marketing has become acute. It is useless to produce unless he can find a profitable market and he must produce the foods which have a ready sale and to some extent are independent of foreign competition. He has this advantage, however, that there is a stability in agriculture which is not found in manufacturing industries.

The maintenance of a rural population is essential for our national life, for if we become too predominantly industrial, and agriculture is thereby restricted, national health and national life must suffer. We cannot judge agriculture purely by economic standards, otherwise we could invoke the doctrine of the survival of the fittest and say they must either survive or succumb. It is therefore not only an economic problem but also a problem for the State, since there are many other aspects of agriculture which require that it should be maintained. In fact, national security and national defence make it necessary for the State to give special consideration to this industry. We see in many countries of the world the determination on the part of Governments, by means of tariffs and subsidies, to maintain and increase a rural population. It is only recently in this country that legislation has been devised with a view to preventing further rural depopulation and enabling the farmer willing to adopt new ideas and modern methods to maintain his hold on the land. While we are trying to raise the standard of health and physique, it is important to remember that the soil and climate of England are both fitted to provide large quantities of those protective foods which the nation requires and to increase the vigour of our people. The more highly urbanized a country, the more prone we are to a high rate of mortality and the less likely we are to be able to resist disease. In face, however, of the danger of war, another consideration has arisen which is regarded by Governments as being still more important. More than half our food supplies are imported, and although the idea of making ourselves self-supporting in time of war is chimerical, yet imperial defence cannot view with equanimity our increasing dependence on imports. It is this argument which is used to justify the encouragement which is given to the farmer in the matter of wheat, beef, bacon, and other foods. In the future if the efforts that are being made to encourage agriculture are to succeed there must be conscious and continuous direction of production and marketing which will enable the farmer to make a fair profit without enriching the middleman or penalizing the consumer.

INDEX